GO HELP THE CHILDREN

& GOD HELP YOU

The Memoirs of Jim Maloof

WITH DOUGLAS E. LOVE

Love Publishing Ink
Illinois

Pictures provided courtesy of the James A. Maloof Family Archives.

Maloof, James A.
Go Help the Children & God Help You: The Memoirs of Jim Maloof /
Jim Maloof with Douglas E. Love

ISBN (10): 0615407757
ISBN (13): 978-0-615-40775-3

Printed in the United States of America
by Multi-Ad of Peoria, Illinois

To the Honorable James Maloof

Mayor James Maloof is not only a credit to our heritage – he is also a credit to mankind in his untiring efforts to save stricken children all over the world.

Jimmy has been with me since I first dreamed of St. Jude Children's Research Hospital and it's great benefactor, The American Lebanese Syrian Associated Charities.

Danny Thomas,
January 20, 1989

Forward

Joseph Campbell once said that a hero is someone who has given his or her life to something bigger than oneself; and that a hero is one who has done something beyond the normal range of achievement and experience.

As understood in those terms, there is no question in my mind that James A. Maloof is a hero.

A real life, living, breathing, American hero.

I don't think we'll ever know the number of lives he has saved by raising millions and millions of dollars for St. Jude Children's Research Hospital.

And it is still harder to fathom the number of lives he has touched by his selfless dedication to finding a cure for childhood cancer.

For every life he has touched it is multiplied tenfold when you include the patient's parents, siblings, grandparents, aunts and uncles; and then there are the neighbors and neighborhood friends, and the teachers and friends at school – and it could go on and on.

If you don't know anything else about Jim Maloof, that's all you need to know. Jim is a difference maker, a participant in life; he lives and loves every moment of being alive.

He has an infectious smile and a disarming wit. He likes people, and he likes to make people happy.

Jim truly found his calling in life in 1957 when he

met entertainer Danny Thomas. Jim and Danny were cut from the same cloth.

They were both first generation Lebanese, from poor, hard-working, immigrant families.

They both had radio shows; and they both performed during the early days of television.

And both received a higher calling: to save lives.

This is a simple story about an uncomplicated man, a throwback from a time when integrity was everything and failure wasn't a word.

Over the years, and to this day, people refer to Jim Maloof as "The Singing Mayor," "Mr. Peoria," and "Mr. St. Jude."

His closest friends and family are known to call him "Your Honor," as in "How are you today, Your Honor."

Philanthropist Wayne Baum simply calls him "The Legend."

And perhaps the biggest compliment of all is that the people on the street still address him as "Mr. Mayor." Jim Maloof hasn't been the mayor of Peoria in over 13 years, but that's what they call him. That's how revered he is.

At 91 years old, if he decided to run for Mayor of Peoria he'd win. He's more popular now then when he was in office.

This book is a composite of ten different interviews I conducted with Jim over the course of two years.

It was Jim's idea to tell his story through vignettes. And these small stories put together make up the whole of his extraordinary life.

He has been a joy and a blessing to work with. And honestly, I didn't know him before I started on this project, but it didn't take long for me to realize that Jim Maloof was an appointed child of God – sent on a mission to accomplish amazing things which no human being could do alone.

Inside you will find the memories and reminiscence of a man who loves his life, loves his family, loves his community, and has been humbled and blessed by his God.

These stories are sure to make you laugh and maybe even make you cry. They are certainly going to touch your heart.

I hope you enjoy them.

Douglas E. Love
Peoria Heights, Illinois
Sunday, August 29, 2010

Introduction

Jim Maloof's story is not so much a Horatio Alger account as a rich telling of a lifetime of devotion. He is surely one of the best-known men in Peoria's long history. He is still "Mr. Mayor" to many of us and a tireless crusader for the St. Jude cause to others. Here, we not only get a slice of that rich history, but a full-blown portrait of a man whose faith has moved mountains, and whose love has had the power to change his world and ours as well.

Jerry Klein,
October 13, 2010

GO HELP THE CHILDREN

& GOD HELP YOU

The Memoirs of Jim Maloof

Contents

BOOK 1

BOOK 2

BOOK 3

BOOK 4

BOOK 5

BOOK 6

Make a Difference

"Lord, may I make a difference in all I do, the words I say, and the actions I take. Lord, May I glorify you, that you might be pleased with me."*

--George Bernard Shaw

*This saying hangs on my wall & I try to live by it.

Prologue

I've been asked so many times to write the story of my life, and I've often wondered, "Well, if I write a book about my life, what would I put in and what could I leave out?"

It's a tough question when you've lived a life as full as mine.

My life has spanned seventeen presidents, starting with Woodrow Wilson; and three times, I was elected Mayor of Peoria, Illinois. I was blessed with the opportunity to travel the world, meet distinguished diplomats and to dine with foreign dignitaries.

I've been to Reagan's White House, and I've met Presidents Nixon, Ford, Carter, and Bush – both father and son.

I served in World War II, and I've served meals at the South Side Mission.

My life has been blessed with a variety of experiences, both good and bad.

But nothing has touched my heart more than the words "go help the children and God help you."

The impact of what those words mean to me cannot be underestimated, for

"Go help the children & God help you"

were the last words that my mother said to me on her death bed at St. Francis Hospital on April 1, 1969.

And it's to her precious memory, I solemnly dedicate this book.

My mother Sarah Zyne Maloof and my father Nimer Marud Maloof

BOOK 1

The Memoirs of Jim Maloof

Book 1: Chapter 1: Inspiration

Well, today is August the 15th which is the celebration of the Assumption of Mary in the Roman Catholic Church.

It is quite ironic that I am to begin the story of my life on this day, because my mother, Sarah, always claimed that August the 15th was her birthday.

My parents, like many immigrants in the late 1800's, had no idea of when their true birth dates were, so they made them up. Not because they liked making such things up, but because there are many times in life when you need a birth date. Like when they were filling out their immigration forms, and census papers, and so on.

My mother loved the Blessed Virgin Mary so much that she wanted this day, more than any other, to be her birthday.

I want to tell you, my mother had such a tremendous influence on me. She was loved by more people than you could imagine. She could not read or write English, but she knew the true meaning of the word "Love." And she taught it to me.

Our first and greatest commandment is *to love God* and *to love our neighbor as ourselves.*

And as a youngster growing up in the migrant section of Peoria during the 1920's, I was keenly aware of how my mother treated other people.

She was always giving, especially to those in the greatest of need, the downtrodden, the hungry and indigent.

During the great depression and into the thirties, I remember people knocking on our door asking for food, and she always invited them in.

As far back as I can remember strangers ate at our table, poor people of every color.

My mother could hardly speak a lick of English, but she could point a finger, and say "You. Eat."

And when my parents owned the dry cleaning business, everyday, she would prepare a 2 gallon tub of lemonade for the workers. She squeezed all the lemons by hand, and she did it everyday. She was a strong woman, inside and out.

Back in those days, we had a coal-fired stove in our kitchen. She didn't cook with gas; she did the laundry by hand; she didn't have a refrigerator; and she didn't have the luxuries that we have today, but she never complained.

My mother was always giving of herself. She was only too happy to help other people. You can imagine why she had such an influence over me, wherever I went, whatever I did.

The only thing I can remember which she didn't want me to do was to become a priest.

Right after I graduated from the eighth grade I went to Cincinnati for a long weekend to think about the priesthood, and, wow, was she upset about that.

Granted, it sounds like a contradiction, a woman so full of love not wanting her son to wear the cloth, but it was less about the profession and more about losing her youngest child.

I clearly remember her saying to me, "You must stay home with your brothers and take care of the family business. We need you."

But as I think back over my life, that was about the only thing she didn't want me to do. Everything else, she encouraged me all along the way.

Book 1: Chapter 2: **Nimer and Sarah**

My parents came to this country with hope. And after being here, they continued on with a firm belief in themselves, a firm belief in God, and a desire to do something for America. A desire to do something for the country that allowed them to come here as immigrants, and to enjoy the liberties of the Bill of Rights and all the goodies that America had to offer.

At the turn of the century, there weren't a lot of jobs available in Lebanon. So, the opportunity to work, that was the main reason my parents wanted to come to America.

My father's name was Nimer: Nimer Maloof. And he was born and raised in Zahle, Lebanon.

Zahle was (and still is) a very, very popular destination – sort of a resort town that sits in this majestic valley, situated at the foot of the mountains. Zahle is famous for its water -crystal clear drinking water- food, fun, and entertainment.

My mother, Sarah Zyne, was born in Fizul, Lebanon, in 1890. I know that because she used to have the year tattooed on the back of her hand. It sounds kind of strange today, but there were no county clerks back then, well, at least not in those parts of Lebanon anyway, so if the parents wanted to keep track of how old their kids were, they would tattoo the year on the back of their hand. And I remember on the back of my mother's hand it said 1890.

My mother was the daughter of Mr. and Mrs. Ibrahim Zyne.

A number of Lebanese people had immigrated to America before my mom or dad got here.

They had heard that the job opportunities in America were great. They heard that the streets in America were not only blacktopped, but paved with gold. And when they got here, of course, they found out they weren't even paved at all. But that didn't distress them, that didn't turn them away. My parents were just grateful to have the opportunity to come to America; to get jobs; to get married; to have, raise, and educate their children here.

However, it should be told that my parents didn't come to America together. In fact, they didn't even know each other in the old country.

My dad came to America first. He came through Ellis Island in 1900. He was a very strong, rugged, 18-year old at the time. I'm under the impression that he took odd jobs doing hard, physical, manual labor somewhere in and around the Brooklyn area.

He had a sister, Adele Lian, who lived in Kings County, New York: Brooklyn. Adele's husband Spiridon and his brother George were highly respected merchants; together, they owned a retail store called Fancy Laces.

There was a little factory nearby, where all the

sewing and embroidery work was done for the shop. My dad's sister-in-law Rebecca, who arrived in 1892, did sewing there.

When my mom, Sarah, arrived in 1905, she also took a little job sewing at the factory.

I just want to mention, I don't actually know who my mom came over with, but it would not have been unusual for a girl to travel with other girls back in those days. You know, just a group of girls traveling alone. You didn't have the threats of being attacked or anything like you do today, it was a different world.

And it was a big commitment on the parents' part to send their child to America, because once they put their child on that boat, they might never see them again.

I don't believe my mom ever saw her parents again; it wasn't uncommon, that's what happened with thousands of young people who were making the voyage to America.

So, anyway, my mom, my dad's sister-in-law Rebecca, my dad's sister Adele, etc..., all of these folks that worked together, lived on the same street together, if not in the same tenement building together. They were all Lebanese, all from the old country, and they were one big family, if they were related or not.

And it was during this time, and immediately after Sarah arrived from Ellis Island, that Nimer stopped over to visit his sister Adele. And much to his surprise, he found out that she had a young lady who was living with her, a beautiful young lady of fifteen, going on sixteen.

My aunt Adele played a little matchmaker or whatnot; Nimer and Sarah met and some months later, wow, they were engaged.

Eventually, they got married in the Bay Ridge section of Brooklyn, in my aunt's kitchen. I always laugh and say, "It must have been some kitchen," because that's where they were married.

My father's Lebanese name, or given name, was Nimer Ibrahim Maloof. My dad, like my mom, couldn't read or write a lick of English. And somewhere between leaving Lebanon and arriving in New York, his name was changed, twice. I think somewhere along the way he said Nimer, and they didn't know that name or how to spell it, so they wrote down Nick, and for whatever reason, it stuck. So, he ended up being Nick Maloof.

Tradition would have it that Nimer, now Nick, should carry his father's first name as his middle name. So, if his father was Ibrahim Marud Maloof, and it was, my dad's name should have been Nick Ibrahim Maloof. Make sense?

Ok, well, somewhere along the line, my dad ended up being Nick Marud Maloof, instead of Nick Ibrahim or even Nick Abraham Maloof. So, he ended up with his grandfather's first name as a middle name, not his dad's. How that got all fouled up, I don't think we'll ever know.

So to make a long story short, my dad spent the rest of his life as Nick Marud Maloof. But everyone just called him Nick.

Members of the Maloof clan started arriving in America at different times, so we all ended up with different names. Some of us are Maloof, others are Maluf; still others spelt their name Malouf, Maaluf,

Maalloof, Malough, Melof, Malooff, Mallof; it goes on and on.

As far as I know, the old country name was Ma'loof.

Anyway, my grandfather Ibrahim Murad Ma'loof was born around 1849. He married Raghe: (and surprise) her name was anglicized to Rachel. She was three years younger than he was.

I don't really know anything about my grandfather, except I remember that we had a picture of him with a big handlebar mustache. That is the only thing I can really remember about him.

I can only guess that he probably died in Lebanon shortly before 1915, because that's when Raghe came to the United States to live with my mom and dad, and he didn't come along.

My parents were married in New York in November of 1907. There they had their first son, which they named after Nimer's father, Abraham. But, of course, they just called the kid Abe.

From there, mom and dad rode the rails west to Peoria, Illinois.

They came to Peoria because there was already an established Lebanese community here: the LaHoods and Couris, the people from Itoo, Lebanon, you know, the one's that founded the ITOO Society, they were already here. And somehow, word must have spread throughout the Lebanese community in New York that there were jobs here, and that there were already other Lebanese people established here. So, my parents moved to Peoria.

Immediately, my dad found work across the river, as a brick maker, in Creve Coeur, Illinois.

Then on November 11, 1909, they welcomed their second son into the world, Mitchell Maloof.

My parents, and two brothers, lived in a small apartment down in the 500 block of South Adams, near the foot of the Franklin Street Bridge.

Everyday, my dad would have to walk across the bridge, along the river where the bottoms were, then cut across over to where the brick factories were. So, he'd walk five miles to work; work ten hours; and at the end of the day walk back home, come snow, rain, sleet, or shine.

And every day, when he arrived home, the house was clean and my mother had dinner ready to eat.

This was America, and life was good.

For many people that came to America, this was the end of their story. They came to America, got jobs, put food on the table, and raised a family.

But it wasn't good enough for my parents. They were determined that their boys would have a better life. They were driven to work harder, save more, and forge ahead.

Book 1: Chapter 5: **Entrepreneurs**

In case you haven't noticed, the Lebanese people in general have a very entrepreneurial spirit. They possess a certain independent frame of mind. And this statement is just as true today as it was back then. And it was certainly true of my parents as well.

While my dad was busy making bricks, my mom started a little job of her own to help the family out.

With whatever little extra money she could accrue, she'd go downtown to the Peoria Dry Goods store or to the old Block and Kuhl; look around; find table cloths, or linen towels, or whatever she could find in fancy goods; and she would buy what she could for a bargain price.

Then, she would go out door-to-door and sell that same merchandise to make a little money. The profit was slight -- it wasn't much, but it helped.

My mother worked hard, and eventually her little business began to grow. It grew to the point where she needed to find some sort of transportation to haul the goods around in.

There was no way my parents could afford a car, and they couldn't drive to boot. Eventually, one of the neighbors lent her a horse and buggy.

So, she would take that horse and buggy out into the neighborhoods with her number one son, Abe, sitting right alongside her, and she'd peddle those linens and tablecloths and things all over town.

Shops and Boys

Our family continued to grow, as my parents had their third son, Fred Maloof, in July of 1916. And with the addition of little Fred, the Lebanese community in Peoria was growing too.

There was an empty store downstairs, under where my parents were living. And I don't know what kind of deal my dad arranged with the owner of the building, but he converted that empty store into a coffee room.

The old Lebanese men would come in, drink their black coffee, smoke their unfiltered cigarettes, and read the newspapers sent over from back home.

My dad was well-liked in the Lebanese community, and it didn't take long before the coffee shop was getting to be a pretty popular place.

The first thing you know, the old guys were complaining, "Hey, we need some kind of entertainment in here."

"What do you want?"

"A pool table."

"A pool table? Okay."

So, my dad converted a part of the coffee shop into a pool room.

That lasted a year or so, until dad came up with the idea of starting a small grocery store.

The pool hall/coffee shop space wasn't going to be

big enough for a grocery store, so he began searching around town for something just a little bit bigger. That's when he found an empty store room at the corner of Wayne Street and Glendale.

Dad signed the lease and they moved. Out of this new locale they sold canned goods and vegetables and whatnot. It wasn't big, but it was big enough for a family store.

Eventually, dad gave up his job as a brick maker. He was now working full time at the grocery store – along with my mom and Raghe.

I think it caught them by surprise, but business improved rather quickly. And it didn't take long before they needed more space.

That's when they moved into 401 W. First Avenue. The new grocery store was on the ground floor, with an apartment located upstairs. This was typical of most family-run businesses in those days.

And it was in this little upstairs apartment at the corner of First Avenue and State Street, in Peoria, Illinois, where I was born.

Legend has it that on October 18, 1919, I greeted life with a song. And I believe that to be true.

My parents named me Jameel Maloof, and I was brought into this world by midwife. Later, my mother had to go into the hospital for repair work, for all the damage I caused her.

I know it sounds like I'm joking, but it's the honest-to-goodness truth.

Book 1: Chapter 7: Childhood Memories

Behind the grocery store at 401 W. First Avenue, was a one bedroom apartment, and upstairs over the grocery store, were four bedrooms. So, my brothers (Abe, Mitchell, and Fred) and my grandma (Raghe), we all lived upstairs in those rooms.

My mom and dad lived downstairs in the grocery store, or, I should say, in the bedroom behind the grocery store.

Raghe was a very simple woman, soft-spoken. She had nice looking gray hair; pretty good size; and about 5'9". She didn't work, but she did help my mother take care of the house. I don't recall her ever getting upset or mad at anything.

But she used to drive us boys bonkers when she'd pinch our cheeks so hard. You know we were babies, and she'd say "Smallah" and pinch your cheek.

Another way of her liking you was to pat you on the cheek. Bam!

Sometimes she'd do it to the neighbor kids, and some of the women would go crazy, "Don't hit my kid!"

One of the sweetest memories I can remember as a small child was that of my mother sitting on the couch listening to records.

In the evenings, when she got done with her chores and supper and after she got the kitchen all cleaned up, she'd come out and sit on the davenport and play her records.

She used to love to listen to those records, and I'd sit there on her lap. And we were so happy. She'd play those records for hours on end. She wasn't a singer, she just loved music.

I'm certain that my love for music came from my mother.

By the early 1920's, my parents' grocery store had grown into a meat market. The meat market had a butcher shop. The meat wasn't pre-wrapped and ready to go for the customer like it is today.

So a customer might come in and say, "Give me six chops off that loin," or "I'll take a piece of round steak off of that butt of steak there."

Then, either mom or dad would have to cut the meat fresh off the bone, weigh it, and wrap it, all while the customers waited.

At the age of 3, in that butcher shop, that's when my singing career actually began. My parents, you see, would stand me on the counter and coax me into singing this little song.

> *"My mother is the butcher,*
> *My father cuts the meat,*
> *And I am the little weenie*
> *That runs around the street."*

You know, it was like a "live" on the spot commercial, the real thing. And if you watch TV commercials today, you know how often babies are used in ads. Maybe I missed my calling; maybe, I was born 88 years too soon?

The customers thought it was cute; it gave my parents some time to get the meat ready; and the people kept coming back, so, hey, maybe I was good for business.

Book 1: Chapter 9: **In the Early Days**

I recall the bathtubs in the early days – until you got to be 8 or 9 or 10 years old – the bathtub was a big round iron bucket. It was about a foot and a half high and about 3 foot in diameter; you couldn't stretch out, you just sat in the water with your legs buckled up.

My mother would have to heat the water for me to take a bath. She'd heat the water over the old coal-burning stove.

I'd sit in there and my mother would scrub me down and let me play in the water and whatever.

Then she would get some kind of a pan or tin cup and fill it with water out of the tub and rinse the soap from my head and off my back.

Back in those days, we had no refrigerators. The iceman would come by the house two or three days a week in the summer.

My mother had a large pantry, maybe 8' x 12', where she kept pots and pans and groceries. Twice a week, my dad would go down to the markets around 4 o'clock in the morning.

And he wouldn't buy a couple of pounds of tomatoes, no, he'd buy the whole box.

He'd also buy a box of lettuce and whatever other veggies they were in need of.

I remember him buying a leg of lamb; he would

bring it home and trim it down: we seldom ate beef in those days. But my mother could make the food taste so good, it was unbelievable.

In our backyard, we had a big 30 gallon tub.

My mother used to kill her own chickens, break their necks and clean them back there.

She'd put hot water in that tub; wring the chicken's neck, wring it until the head came off; and then dump the body in the hot water.

The hot water loosened up the feathers, and after awhile, she'd take them out and pluck the feathers off.

Then she'd cut out the insides, cut the gizzards out and get all that stuff. Then come back inside and cook it.

Book 1: Chapter 10: **Sacred Heart**

In 1924 I started school. I was enrolled at Sacred Heart, which was located on the corner of Fulton and Madison. It's where the church is now.

There was no such thing as kindergarten; so naturally, I started in first grade at the age of 6.

The school was run by a Franciscan priest (the principal) and by the Franciscan nuns (the teachers).

The nuns there were heavy on singing, serving mass, and teaching Latin. We learned a lot from the nuns, but, boy, were they tough on discipline.

My, my, I recall, it was in either the first or second grade, I was a left-hander, and this nun was going to teach me how to write right-handed; she put my left arm behind my back, and using a big safety pin, she pinned the sleeve of my left arm to the back of my shirt, in effect, forcing me to write right-handed.

It's not the worst handwriting in the world these days, but that was one of the ways of doing things "their way."

We went through Confirmation in the sixth or seventh grade. It was probably the seventh grade. But anyway, there were thirteen kids in our class: seven boys and six girls.

And the nuns, they had such an influence on us,

that all seven boys took the name Aloysius (pronounced al'-uh-WISH-us): after Aloysius Gonzaga, the patron saint of children.

So, I became Jameel Aloysius Maloof. And in retrospect, how fitting is that, the patron saint of children.

But as I think back, I believe that by the time I left first grade, my name had all ready been changed to James, and shortly after that people were calling me Jim.

And after that, and I can't help but laugh because it's true, but after that they were calling me "Big Mouth," and that's the way it's been since I can remember.

Another thing that goes back to my earlier education is the answer to a question people often ask me, "How in the heck do you remember so many darn songs?"

Well, starting in the sixth grade, the nuns used to enter me into the city-wide spelling bees.

Back then we had no spelling lists to go over, so every morning the nun would bring a newspaper to school. She'd have the words for that day underlined or circled.

During recess, sometimes during lunch, and at other times after school, I would have to memorize and recite the words she had underlined in the newspaper. And then later on, she'd have someone test me on those words.

I never won a spelling bee, but it got to the point to where I think it improved my memory.

And I really believe that.

I used to walk to school, until I got my bike.

There was a place over on Franklin Street, three blocks away, called Voss Brothers, they were a bicycle shop.

I don't know how I managed to save the money, but for $14 dollars I bought a Peoria King bicycle.

It didn't have any bells or whistles or anything, just a seat big enough for my butt.

But boy, was I big man on the block with my new bicycle.

That was a big day in my life, to buy and own my own bicycle. It was a part of my upbringing. My parents wanted me to learn that if I wanted something worthwhile, and if I wanted it bad enough, then I needed to start working for it.

I had to save, there were no charge accounts. That was the lesson, you know, when you go and get it you pay for it in full.

I think it was that same discipline that just transformed my whole life.

And on a side note here, remember the old men hanging out in the coffee shop, well in 1924 they started their own little club called The American Lebanese Syrian Society (ALSS). I mention it here, because it will come up again later.

But, the concept of the ALSS was to honor and preserve our Lebanese-Syrian heritage. And both of my parents were active members.

Regrets I've Had a Few

At home my parents tried to teach us Lebanese. And in the early years, they only spoke Lebanese themselves.

So, I learned to understand what they were saying, but to speak it, that was another ball of wax.

And, honestly, as a kid, I wasn't really too interested in learning to read and write Arabic, it didn't seem too important.

I mean, I was going to a school where the American language was number one. You didn't have a choice, you learned to read and write English.

Plus, at that age, it was more important for me to play ball, study for the spelling bee, or spend my free time singing. Those things were more important to me than learning Arabic.

My parents, on the other hand, being in business, were sort-of forced to learn English. Yeah, they spoke broken English, but they had to learn the language to keep their business afloat. And I give them a lot of credit for that.

But as for myself, to this day, I still regret not having learned to speak the Lebanese language.

Book 1: Chapter 12: It Just Takes Soap and Water

At the back of the grocery store, there was another little room, maybe 10' x 10'. And my dad, I don't know where he learned it or if he taught himself, but he started using this space to repair oriental rugs. Now, oriental rugs were a big item in those days because people didn't have tacked down carpeting back then.

And being the entrepreneur he was, word got out:

"Nick Maloof, oriental rug repairman"

And the next thing you know, people are stopping by the grocery store saying, "Hey, Nick, can you repair my rug?"

"Oh, sure," he'd say. "I can fix anything." Or at least, he'd try to fix anything. My dad wasn't one to say "no."

And this is how he'd clean those rugs.

There was a driveway between the store and the house next door. Dad would take the rugs out, not in the winter, but in the summer, and rinse them out with water; squeegee off the old; put some soap on them; scrub them by hand; squeegee them off again; and then try to dry them with this vacuum kind of thing. And after that, he'd bring them back in and hang them up to finish drying.

So, that's basically how he got started in the rug

---

cleaning business, with a clothes line, a brush, some soap and water.

It was a simple lesson for me to learn, but an important one. From watching my parents, I came to understand that if you want to do something in this world, you find a way to do it.

Tough Neighborhood

The grocery store had half bushel baskets of peppers and tomatoes and cucumbers and things out in front of the store.

Rarely did anybody ever try to steal them.

Occasionally, a kid would run by and try to take something and go running off, but that was the exception. And we had quite a bit of traffic in those days, we were only four blocks from downtown Peoria.

Right behind the grocery store was the kitchen and then the staircase which led upstairs.

My mother and I were eating one day, I must've been about 5 or 6-years old, when she heard the register.

"Bing."

She went to the top of the stairs and, looking down into the grocery store, saw a guy trying to steal the money out of the drawer.

She yelled down, "You don't take money from register."

Then she started down towards him. I stayed at the top of the stairs watching.

"Put it back or I hit you," she said to him.

"You git out of har-r," the guy said. His speech was somewhat slurred, he was a bit drunk I guessed.

My mother then said, "I tell you one more time. Put back. You want to eat, I feed you. Don't take money."

He paid no attention.

"Put back," she said again.

"Shut up," he yelled.

At that, she grabbed Raghe's cane which had been left by the counter, it was a 4-foot stick, and with it she started beating the thief.

"Put money back, no?" she asked in between blows.

He fell down, and she kept beating him.

He started crawling from the back of the store, clear up to the front door. And by now she had hit him so many times, he was bleeding.

As he neared the door, she yelled up to me, "Tell Mrs. Karbage, call police! Call police!" Mrs. Karbage was our neighbor.

I remember so clearly, she put her foot on his head and said, "Damn you, don't you move. I kill you. You take money, when I offer to feed you. I told you, don't take money."

And the man never got up again until the police came.

Her arms were stronger than the Cedars of Lebanon. She was a robust woman: fearless.

Another time, I was sitting on the couch with our Doberman Pincer, Asta.

Now, Dobermans are kind of one-person dogs. And Asta was my mother's dog. No question about it, that dog loved my mother.

And, boy, let me tell you, if you looked cross-eyed

that dog was after you. That happened to me once or twice: that dog was something else.

Anyway, one night, we were sitting in the living room when a guy came up on the front porch. I think he was looking for a house of prostitution, which were all around the neighborhood.

My mother went to the door, and the guy says, "I want a woman."

"No woman here," she said, "get out."

And he said to her, "Now lady, get away, I'm coming in. I want a woman."

"I tell you get out. Get out or you'll be sorry."

And by now the dog is right at her feet.

"Get," she said for a third time.

And the guy wouldn't listen. He opened the screen door and my mother yelled, "Get him Asta."

That dog bolted forward and was all over that guy in a split second.

He tried to get away from the dog, but fell down. There were 5 cement steps, and the guy and dog tumbled down them. Oh, my heavens, you should have seen it.

Asta bit him and tore open his flesh a few times.

The guy got up to run, and that dog chased him all the way down the street.

My mom yelled after him, "Asta. STOP!" And that dog listened to her, and came right back home.

If she hadn't of done that, Asta would have chewed that guys head off.

A lot of the Lebanese men made their own alcohol, and my dad was no exception.

He used to make this drink called Mastika-Ada. It was moonshine, like white lightning. It was 180 proof. In Greek Mastika means *to gnash the teeth.* You get idea.

Us kids didn't know about his distillery until much later, because he hid it down in the basement.

He would take fresh grapes, just like the Italians make their wine, but he would take white grapes and boil them. Their fumes used to go up a pipe and over then into a gallon jug. Then as it cooled, it became this powerful drink.

Usually, it was poured over ice and had with mezedes, or appetizers.

Three times a day my dad would drink that: morning, noon, and night.

And when his friends were over, sometimes they'd get so loud.

And they had a hookah pipe – a water pipe. I don't know what they smoked in it, some kind of tobacco from the old country.

Guess who used to smoke from that water pipe?

My mother, can you believe that. But it was acceptable for a Lebanese woman to do that back then. These were the ways of the old country.

Robert Livingston and I met in the summer of 1933, shortly after I returned from Cincinnati. If you remember, I had gone to Cincinnati to contemplate the priesthood.

My mother had said "no" to the priesthood, but "okay" to summer camp – because she knew, no one stays at summer camp indefinitely.

And that's where we met, Livy and I, up there at St. Bede's Academy in Peru, Illinois.

Livy, that's what everybody called Robert, not Bob or Bobby, no, it was just Livy, short for Livingston of course.

And Oh Heavens, what a good time that camp was. We ate there, slept there, played games, and so forth, for a whole week. I remember it was a lot of fun.

Livy had just graduated from St. Bernard's, and I had just graduated from Sacred Heart.

As it turned out, both of us loved sports, and frequently we found ourselves competing against each other. It was this healthy competition, a kind of respect we had for each other that really made our friendship.

That fall, we ended up starting Spalding together as freshmen.

And I must admit, Livy was better than I was in darn near everything.

We were on the golf team together, and he was better.

We were on the baseball team together, and he was better.

He excelled at music, at art, and athletics. And he did it in such a way that it wasn't a braggadocio kind of thing. He was just a genuine, talented, all around good guy.

And he had such a wonderful voice. We sang together the entire four years at Spalding, so I know.

After high school, Livy went on study at St. Meinrad's over in Indiana. And it was Livy who became the priest.

The priests in those diocese, where he worked, regarded Father Livingston as a Priest's Priest because of his demeanor, his compassion and understanding. He was capable of doing anything, and yet so willing to help anybody.

I had so much respect for him, and watching him make something out of his life had such a significant impact on mine.

I wish I had the words to tell you just how special a person he was, because he was exceptional. And, honestly, just being around him made me a better person.

We graduated 37 kids from Spalding Institute in 1937.

Thirty-seven in '37, as we like to say. And it was a pretty good class.

Livy went on to become a highly respected member of the clergy, while Bob Lehnhausen, who'd also gone to St. Bernard's, became the Mayor of Peoria in 1965. And I became the Mayor of Peoria twenty years later in 1985.

One guy became a naval commander; and another became some kind of scientific engineer.

I think overall our teachers would have been proud of us.

A lot happened during those middle school to high school years.

If you remember my dad's sister-in-law Rebecca had been working in New York, sewing for Adele Lian's Fancy Laces. Well, she was now widowed and had come to live with us. She shared a room with Grandma Raghe, until Grandma passed away in 1930.

My oldest brother Abe had moved to Indianapolis to study law. My other older brother, Mitchell, had moved out and gotten married.

Mom and dad finally gave up the grocery store, and they went 100% into the rug cleaning business. They moved the business next door, across the driveway, to 403 W. First.

Meanwhile, we continued living at 401 W. First – which my parents now owned.

That's right, my parents who came to this country with nothing, now owned a house. Imagine that.

We had a little more space now and that little 10' x 10' became the kitchen.

Fred, and I, well, we continued to live upstairs with our Aunt Rebecca.

We still had no furnace in the winter; no refrigeration in the summer.

But who could complain, we now had a business and a house.

One of the happiest memories with my parents, back in this time, and we're talking about the 30's and early 40's, is when we all played cards together.

Families played a lot of card games together in those days, we still didn't have television yet.

So, we'd play Pinochle, Bridge, Hearts, Crazy 8's, whatever. Those are some of the games we played.

And playing those games with my dad and his friends and all, you know, just great memories.

But while you are playing cards, you also learned too.

Playing cards is an art. You have to remember the cards, what has been played, what has not been played, it's darn near a business, and it is in Vegas today, isn't it?

Oh yeah, in high school, I wasn't big enough to play basketball, and my mother wouldn't let me play football, she thought I'd get hurt, so I became a cheerleader.

It was also during this time that my parents began the transition from Rug Cleaners to Dry Cleaners – for quite some time we did both.

In high school, I wanted to play ball, and hang out with my friends. I didn't want to go to work. Especially when the weather was warm and it was hot outside.

A lot of times I'd get in trouble with my parents because I wouldn't come straight home from school.

At Spalding, school got out at 3:00 or 3:15 p.m.

And my parents would always be telling me, "You'd better be home by 3:30 p.m."

And I had a bicycle, so I really didn't have any good excuse to be late.

But it wouldn't be unusual for them to find me hanging out somewhere, you know, not causing trouble, just having fun.

If I was missing too long, then they'd send the rug truck out looking for me, and that's when I knew I was in big trouble.

But who could blame me, cleaning rugs was hard work.

I often use the expression, "We slaved." We absolutely slaved. And that's not an over exaggeration.

Remember, almost nobody had tacked down carpeting back then, it was all loose carpeting, or rugs.

So it was like this, first a call would come in, "Come clean my rug."

"Ok."

And you'd drive the rug truck over to the house.

Then you'd get inside; most of the time the rug filled the whole room, wall-to-wall, that was just the way people did it back then.

So, the first thing you did was move all the furniture to one side of the room.

And then you'd start rolling the rug up. And when you got about halfway through, you'd have to pick up all the furniture and move it to the other side of the room.

Sometimes you had help, and a lot of times you did it by yourself.

Once you got the rug all rolled up, you had to get it in the truck.

That doesn't sound too hard, but some of these rugs took two and sometimes three people to pick them up, and sometimes you had to do it all by yourself.

After the rug was loaded on the truck, you still had to go back inside and put all their furniture back just like it was.

This wasn't light weight furniture either it was all real furniture, made out of heavy wood.

And all that work, that was just part of the service.

For a 9' x 12' rug, the business used to get paid $2.50 for picking up it up, cleaning it, drying it, and delivering it back to the house – where you had to move all their furniture again to put the rug back on the floor.

Oh, Lord knows it was tough, and what did I get paid?

Less than 30 cents an hour.

Book 1: Chapter 18: **The Rug Beater**

I don't know where my dad was able to get his hands on this big rug beater, but he bought one.

"Now we we're in the modern world," or so we thought.

It was a simple machine. It worked like a conveyer. You placed the rug in there, and as it went through the machine, these heavy leather straps would beat the dust out of the rug.

And that was one of my jobs. I'd watch the rug, and just when it got to the other side, I'd reverse the wheels, and the rug would come back the other way.

And this was a big, big contraption. But, sometimes we'd have so many rugs on a truck that you couldn't fit them all in the rug beater at the same time.

And the dust? Where did it go?

There was a vacuum underneath that was supposed to suck all the dirt up, but I'm sure I inhaled most of it. When I think about it, goodness' sake, it'd be a health hazard today.

Anyway, once you had them all dusted, you'd carry them out to the garage, where the rug scrubbing room was. We used to make our own rug soap, by the way. Any anyway, you'd rinse it down, then scrub it down, squeegee it by hand, scrape the soap off the rug, get the hose out, rinse it, turn it over, rinse it, squeegee it again, rinse it and ta-dum, it was ready to hang up to dry.

More or less, the same way dad did it when he started.

Later we got a rug ringer.

It'd take two people to pick up a wet rug, they'd weigh about 200 pounds, and we'd run them through this rug ringer.

Once it went through the ringer, you'd carry it to the next room, which was heated. This was the drying room.

There were pipes on the wall, steam pipes. Those steam pipes were run by a water boiler that was coal fed.

And so now, once the dry room is heated, you'd take the rug in there, and there must have been about twenty-five poles in there. These poles had little nails sticking out of them, so you'd hang the rug up on these little nails.

It took sometimes a day and a half, or two days, to dry a rug, depending on how hot the room was. And you'd have fans going too.

Then when it was dry, you'd take it to the front of the store and have someone trim the fringes.

It was just a never-ending job. It was tough.

And most people didn't have their rugs cleaned frequently, so when you cleaned them they were dirty: I mean dirty.

I tell you it was just horrible work.

Certain events in our lives occur like minor miracles.

I want you to know that I don't believe in coincidence, but that God is the guiding force and power behind all things that happen in our lives.

By the summer of 1939, there was nothing extraordinary happening in my life. I'd been out of school for two years now; my best friend, Livy, had gone off to seminary in Indiana; and I was either hauling carpets, sucking dirt, or playing ball.

I was playing softball for Gipps Brewing.

For those youngsters out there that don't know, Gipps Beer was the Bud Light of the beer industry back in those days. They were world famous for their "Amberlin" beer. They shut down, of course, during prohibition, but reopened in the thirties.

The brewery was right down underneath the Franklin Street Bridge. And now, I was the first baseman for the Gipps fast-pitch softball team.

I just loved fast-pitch softball because there was so much action. It was quick action; you had to be on your toes every second because there was always something happening.

And what happened next, I'll never forget. It was

a hot summer day at the ball park when I first met Gertrude M. Burson, the daughter of Eli and Marie Elizabeth Burson.

Gertrude, or Trudy as she liked to be called, had recently moved across the river from Pekin.

Her dad had a steady job in town working as a repairman for the railroad, fixing railcars and the like. But I guess he wasn't making enough to feed and cloth six kids.

So, shortly after Trudy finished her sophomore year of high school, it was decided that she'd move to Peoria to live with her Aunt Bea. Bea Starcevic.

Aunt Bea helped her get a job. And that summer, Trudy started working at the Bee Hive restaurant, a popular little diner on the corner of Main and Jefferson.

The Starcevic's lived over by Woodruff high school, up on North Madison. The house was bigger than the one in Pekin, but it was still a little crowded, as Aunt Bea already had four sons living at home. Their names were Perk, Joe, Bob, and Chet.

Now, Perk, Joe, Chet and I had long been friends. In fact, we all played on the Gipps softball team together.

When Trudy wasn't working, she'd stop down to the park to watch her cousins play ball.

One day, Joe said, "Jim, you've got to meet our cousin."

Along with a passion for softball, I loved to dance, and the Starcevich brothers knew that. Trudy, they told me, also loved to dance.

The next time she showed up at the park, the

cousins called her down from the bleachers, and we were introduced.

We stood talking as a group at first, then, we found ourselves standing there alone.

"You like to dance?" I asked her.

"Yeah."

"Well, there's a dance going on over at the Waterworks Pavilion tonight."

"Where's that?"

"Right there at the corner of Grandview Drive and Galena Road. Joe knows where it's at. Why don't we meet up there tonight?"

And so the first date was made. We met up that night as planned, and we danced and danced and danced. She was sixteen and I was twenty.

It was love at first sight.

And I found out that night that Trudy Burson was absolutely the best dancer in the city of Peoria.

Book 1: Chapter 20: **Romancing and Dancing**

In those days, dancing was a national pastime.

I'd pick Trudy up in the old cleaning truck. We didn't have a passenger car back then, so that's how we romanced, in the old cleaning truck.

I'd pick her up and we'd go to the Inglaterra Ballroom, the National Roof Garden, or head back down to the Waterworks Pavilion.

It didn't take long before Trudy had gained quite some reputation for herself.

And heck, as soon as we'd get there, the guys were lining up, "Hey Trudy, save me a dance," and then another, "Save me a dance."

And that's exactly what was happening. She'd have them lined up all of the time. It was getting harder and harder for me to spend time with her.

There were times too, when a couple would just clear the floor – everybody else would just back off and watch them. That always seemed to be the case when Trudy and Russell Buchen hit the floor.

Russell worked at the dry cleaning shop, and we were very good friends. He had a reputation as a great golfer and an even better dancer. He was a big guy at 6'3", he was very loose and fluid, and when he danced everybody watched.

So, naturally, all the girls lined up to dance with him.

The trouble was he loved to dance with Trudy. And when they were out there dancing, I'd think to myself, "He's out there dancing with my girl. I've just got to get better!"

Book 1: Chapter 21: The Engagement

Well, my competitive nature pushed me to become
the best dancer I could be, and eventually, I became
Trudy's only dancing partner (most of the time).

We dated for two years, which eventually lead to
our engagement. When I gave her the ring, I sang to her
"I'll be with you in Apple Blossom Time."

Ah, it was really romantic – I suppose you had to
be there.

Anyway, there was one small problem to solve
before we could get married – winning over my parents.

Trudy, as sweet as she was, was not Lebanese.
And that was a problem, a big problem, for my mom and
dad. They were from the old country, we might even call
them old school. There was no way they were going to
let their son marry anyone who was not Lebanese.

In those days, it was a common belief, not just for
the Lebanese, but for other nationalities as well, that
you marry within your own kind. Italians were to marry
Italians, Germans to marry Germans, and Lebanese were
to marry Lebanese. Period.

Otherwise, what was the point to preserving our
heritage; and what was the point of the ALSS? Or any
other ethnic club one would belong to, if you were just
going to mix your gene pool?

But Trudy was vivacious, effervescent, and full of
life, and needless to say, it didn't take long before she

won them over. And not just my parents, she eventually won over the whole Lebanese community.

Winning over my parents was the first hurdle. The second, she wasn't Catholic either. So, Trudy ended up having to go through all the special instruction to be accepted by the church.

And, God Bless her, she managed to smile through it all: and then, the date was finally set.

THE WHITE HOUSE
WASHINGTON, D.C.

October 18, 1985

e Honorable James A. Maloof
yor, City of Peoria
om 207, City Hall Building
19 Fulton Street
eoria, Illinois 61602

Dear Jim:

Congratulations and best wishes on your birthday.

May you enjoy many more in the future.

Your friend,

Ronnie Reagan

"I've been to Reagan's White House, and I've met Presidents Nixon, Ford, Carter, and Bush - both father and son."

above: (right to left) Congressman **Bob Michel**, Mayor **Jim Maloof**,
and **General & Mrs. John M. Shalikashvili**.
Shalikashvili served as Chairman of the Joint Chiefs of Staff from 1993-1997.

Jim *(c)* gives some friendly advice to presidential hopeful **Bob Dole** *(r)*.

above: **Jim** and **Trudy Maloof** with President **George H. W. Bush** and the First Lady **Barbara Bush**.

right: **Jim** with President **Gerald Ford**. for the first time. They would meet again some twenty years later.

above: The Bob Michel Bridge Opening, December 16, 1993. *left to right,*
front row: **Trudy and Jim Maloof**, Governor **Jim Edgar**, and Congressman **Bob Michel**.
back row: Senator **Dale Risinger**, **John Ackerman**, and State Rep. **David Leitch**.

Jim Maloof receives a medallion from **C. Everett Koop**, U.S. Surgeon General (1982-1989).

above: (left to right) **Mrs. James A. Maloof (Trudy), Mrs. James Edgar (Brenda), Mrs. George H. W. Bush (Barbara)**, and **Mrs. Robert H. Michel (Corrine)**.

James A. Maloof, Mayor of Peoria, Illinois (1985-1997); **Raymond G. Becker; George H. W. Bush**, the 43rd President of the United States (1989-1993); and **James R. Thompson**, Governor of Illinois (1977-1991).

My Mother ~ a friend to all

Sarah Maloof with baby **Michael** *(Jim and Trudy's first child)*.
This is a rare snapshot of Jim's mother was taken early in the spring of 1943.

> *"I don't believe my mom ever saw her parents again; it wasn't uncommon, that's what happened with thousands and thousands of young people who were making the voyage to America."*

Mr. & Mrs. Nimer Maloof

Jim's parents: **Sarah Zyne Maloof** and **Nimer Marud Maloof**.
This photograph was taken in 1957 on their 50th wedding anniversary.

Sacred

Heart

Jim attended **Sacred Heart** school, located on the corner of Fulton and Madison, from 1924-1933.

right: This old postcard shows what Sacred Heart looked like back in 1931.

It was here that he adopted the name Aloysius - after Aloysius Gonzaga, *the patron saint of children.*

SACRED HEART CHURCH, PEORIA, ILL.—31

JAMES ALOYSIUS MALOOF
Spalding Institute 1937

Father

Robert

Livingston

Friendships of a lifetime

Bishop

Edward

O'Rourke

above: **Trudy Burson Maloof** with son Michael circa 1944.

right: While dating Jim Maloof and Trudy Burson attended this 1939 Christmas Night peformance of Tommy Dorsey at the Inglaterra Ballroom.

"In those days, dancing was a national pastime.

I'd pick Trudy up in the old cleaning truck ... and we'd go to the Inglaterra Ballroom, the National Roof Garden, or head back down to the Waterworks Pavilion."

The Army Air Corps 1943-1945

Jim was stationed at Windsor Locks Army Air Force in Windsor Locks, Connecticut.

(Windsor Locks was renamed Bradley Airfield, after a fallen comrade, on Jan. 20, 1942; however, at this time it was still commonly referred to as Windsor Locks by the personnel.)

IBU5GI02-9(3-5-45)BASE BOWLIN
TEAMS   BRADLEY FLD. CONN

above on left **Jim Maloof** is the third from the left. *above on right:* close up of Jim from same photo.
middle: Jim, seated second from left, is laughing so hard he's almost in tears.
below: Jim can be seen just over the shoulder of the guy about to drink.

above: *(seated)* Private **Jim Maloof**, working in the Army Air Corps personnel department, stamps a transfer order.

below: **Jim** takes a rare moment to relax at home.
"I don't know how I had time to make kids when I was as active as I was," he joked.

MICHAEL MALOOF

MARK MALOOF

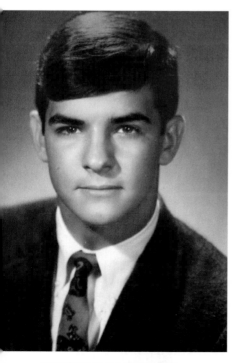

NICK MALOOF

JANICE MALOOF

The children of Jim and Trudy Maloof

Jim and Trudy Maloof

"It was love at first sight."

Book 1: Chapter 22: The Wedding

As is the custom, the Lebanese women in the community, about a dozen of them, would cook for three full days, preparing tons of food and goodies for the big wedding celebration.

On the morning of the wedding, I put on my brand new $19 dollar white linen suit. Trudy slid into a very expensive, very fancy, $35 dollar wedding dress.

The Burson's and Maloof's met at Sacred Heart Church for an 8 a.m. mass (wedding), and then walked over to the Père Marquette Hotel for a wedding breakfast.

We wrapped up breakfast sometime around 11 a.m. and headed to our new apartment.

I had bought, although not yet paid for, enough furniture for a cozy little upstairs apartment over my parent's home at 401 W. First Avenue; rent was $12 dollars a month.

It had one bath; one bedroom, complete with one bedroom set; one small living room, complete with one small living room set; and one kitchen, complete with kitchen set; and a refrigerator and an ice box.

When we got home, there were several women downstairs cooking away, making even more food: it's the Lebanese way.

Trudy slipped out of her wedding dress, put an apron on over her clothes; jumped right in and started helping prepare the food that would be served that night.

I hung up my suit and put on my work clothes. I went next door and worked from about 11:15 a.m. until sometime right around 5 p.m. The shop was busy, making it a long, hot day.

After I got off work, I got cleaned up. Trudy was already waiting for me. I jumped back into my suit, and we rushed over to the wedding reception.

The reception was in an old school house over in the 900 block of South Jefferson which was at this point the American Lebanese Syrian Society clubhouse. By the time we got there it was probably close to 6:30 p.m.

There was plenty to eat and drink. Of course, it was quite an ordeal. There were people wall to wall; dancing; singing; and a lot of speeches given. My brother Mitchell, who was the best man, gave the first toast of the night.

There was all that good stuff, and before we knew it 11 p.m. had rolled around.

"Honey," I said, "we'd better get out of here."

We had a room reserved in LaSalle, Illinois, at the LaSalle Hotel. A friend of mine ran that place up there.

By the time we got out of the reception, and got done kissing everybody goodbye, it was going on midnight.

We ran home and changed clothes as quickly as we could.

I had borrowed by brother's car; it had a full tank of gas and was all set to go. I had about $125 dollars in my pocket and I was feeling fat, fat rich, with a lovely, lovely, new bride by my side. I was on top of the world.

But for all the excitement, I could feel myself

growing tired. I'd already put in 18 hours of wedding, and work, a long with that night's celebration. I was feeling beat.

And I still had to make the drive to LaSalle.

As we climbed in the car, I said to her, "Trudy, now look, I'm pretty darn tired here. I know you can't drive," –she hadn't learned to drive yet- "but if I get sleepy, we are going to pull off the road and get a little rest, and then head on out up to LaSalle."

Well, we only got as far as Metamora, when my eyes just wouldn't stay open. I pulled off to the side of the road and took a short nap. Trudy laid her head on my shoulder, and snuggled up close to me.

It was about two-thirty in the morning when we finally rolled in to LaSalle. And when we finally strolled in to the LaSalle Hotel, there wasn't a soul in the place, except the clerk behind the counter.

And as we were checking in, a big voice came out of the back of the hotel lobby.

"Maloof! Maloof! I knew it! I just knew it!," said the hotel's owner, "You're shacking up with that little broad from Pekin."

"No," I said. "Look, we're married. We're on our honeymoon."

"Come on," he roared, "you're shacking up with her."

"No. No. No," I protested, but he wouldn't shut up until I showed him our wedding certificate.

Trudy just about died.

Book 1: Chapter 23: **The World Changes**

Trudy and I married on June 28, 1941. But it didn't take long before our world changed.

On December 7, the Japanese bombed Pearl Harbor. And almost immediately, my brother Fred enlisted in the U.S. Army.

Trudy was pregnant now.

And on October 11, 1942, we welcomed our first child into the world, Michael.

And, wow, are there a lot of things to learn when you don't know much about little babies. Like how little they sleep and how much they cry and of, course, you don't know why. All that fun stuff young couples go through, we were experiencing ourselves. In the throes of life we were!

And as the war progressed, Uncle Sam put out the call for more young men to join the war effort.

I don't know what caused him to do it, but my brother Mitchell went to the draft board and said, "Look, we've got a problem ... we've got a business to run ... I'll enlist if you make sure my baby brother gets to stay home and keep the family business open."

I guess the draft board said, "Okay" or whatever, or "until the need gets too great."

If you remember, our oldest brother Abe, had already moved to Indianapolis to practice law.

So, if Mitchell signed up, I was the only family left to help mom and dad run the store.

Mitchell signed up in '42. And by August of '43, the war had gotten worse and Uncle Sam sent a letter saying "you must come into the service," which I did willingly.

It broke my heart to tell my parents, because by that time, I was putting in maybe 18 hours a day. I was doing everything from dry cleaning to spotting, to pressing, to cleaning rugs, to pick up and delivery. There was hardly any help.

So I had to ask, "Dad, what are we going to do with the place?"

You have to understand that, basically, everybody that was either young or healthy had already entered the service.

So, finally, we decided to close the business down. There just weren't enough workers or young people in Peoria left to run it.

Book 1: Chapter 24: The Army Air Corps

At the station, after kissing Trudy goodbye, I caught the train to Chicago.

I had been drafted into the army, but somehow I kind of talked myself into letting them make me a part of the newly formed Army Air Corps.

The transfer from the regular army to the Army Air Corps meant that I'd be going down to Miami Beach for basic training.

It was a long train ride, and we arrived at around two in the morning. I remember there were about 500 young recruits, all standing in front of our barracks.

We were inspected by a corporal by the name of Rubin. He was a rough and tumble type.

"I can't hear you."

"Yes, sir," some guy would holler out.

To which Corporal Rubin would stare him down, then cruise down the line.

At some point, he bellowed out, "All right, can anybody in this group sing? Is there anybody here who thinks he can sing?"

I don't know why, but immediately I put my hand out.

"Come out here," he barked, pointing to the spot where he wanted me to stand.

"Private James Maloof, sir."

"All right private," he said, "I'm going to see if you can learn some songs, and if you can sing good enough you are going to become the song leader for the squadron."

I managed to pass Corporal Rubin's inspection and became the song leader, which was kind of a big deal, because in the Army Air Corps in those days you sang whenever you marched, and you sang in unison all the way.

> Here's a toast to the host
> Of those who love the vastness of the sky,
> To a friend we send a message of his brother men who fly.
> We drink to those who gave their all of old,
> Then down we roar to score the rainbow's pot of gold.
> A toast to the host of men we boast, the U.S. Air Force!

You know, some little diddy like that; not that clean though, again, I'm laughing, but it's true.

We must've been pretty good though, because three times we won the title of the best singing group in the Air Corps, but the people in Miami were not too happy with us.

We would leave our barracks about six in the morning. We'd march for about a mile and a half or 2 miles to Bayfront Park where we did our training. On the way over, as we passed by the houses, apartments, and hotels, through the streets of Miami we would sing.

And we used to get all kinds of notes from the residents there saying, "Quit the doggone singing," among other things. Naturally, the more of those notes we received, the louder we would sing.

Oh my, we had a lot of fun doing that.

But then on the last day of basic training in Miami Beach, I hurt my knee and had to have surgery.

They wanted to send me home, but I said, "No. No. No."

And so they sent me to Windsor Locks, Connecticut, about 10 miles north of Hartford.

And because of my knee, they gave me a desk job.

Right away, I was shuffling papers in the personnel department.

It might sound like I landed a posh job, but it wasn't as easy as you might think.

Whenever we got orders from headquarters that said we needed 60 or 80 or 100 personnel of various classifications, it was my job to select those people.

Oh boy, it was tough knowing I was responsible for sending kids, 18, 19, 20 years old into the war zones. Knowing deep down inside that a good number of them would be captured, or injured or even killed.

As I said, it was my job to put them up for transfer. And as I filled out the paperwork, I would start to wonder if this "Joe" had a wife or kids back home. Then my mind would drift and I would start thinking of Trudy and Michael. And that's when I realized, I didn't want to know if this guy had a wife or kids back home. I tried hard not to think about those things.

It was very trying on me. It was tough, honestly, at times it was just about enough to drive me nuts.

I felt so bad, so responsible, that a couple of times I went to the base Colonel, a Colonel Johnson, and asked to be sent over to fight in the European Theatre. "You're fighting the war in a different way," he said.

I know at least three times I asked him, he wouldn't let me go.

I got a little letter from back home saying that my dad had opened a little ice cream parlor.

Across the street from us, there used to be a barbershop run by Nelson Firebaugh. And I guess, sometime after I'd gone into the service, old Nel had went out of business.

So my dad decided to open a little ice cream parlor where that barbershop used to be.

I mean, why not? It only took one person to run it. And all he needed was a couple of tables and chairs, so it wasn't a very big investment.

There were still kids in the neighborhood, you know, and who doesn't like ice cream?

And heck, dad wasn't going to sit around and do nothing, just because there was a war going on.

Singing With Glenn Miller

If sending boys into the war zone was the lowest point of my military career, the highlight had to be when I was asked to sing with the Glenn Miller Army Air Force Band.

The Glenn Miller Orchestra, of course, had been huge back in the late thirties and early forties. They had hits like *Tuxedo Junction, Moonlight Serenade,* and *In the Mood,* along with many others. I mean Glenn Miller was it.

But at the peak of his career, he signed up for active duty. I think everyone was shocked, but that's what he wanted to do, so, okay by me.

Anyway, he was on his way to Europe to entertain the troops over there, but first, he stopped by Windsor Locks Army Air Corps base.

I'm not sure how it all happened, it was such a whirlwind, but somebody had arranged for me to get up on stage and sing with Glenn Miller and his Air Force Band.

Let me tell you, it was unbelievable. With Glenn Miller behind me, and a few thousand faces in front of me, it was like living in a dream. I felt so incredibly honored, and I had a blast.

As far as I know, it was the last time Glenn Miller performed in the United States: Just few months later his plane disappeared over the English Channel. Nobody knows what happened to him?

Singing for Glenn Miller added a new dimension to my singing career. And so did this, I sang for my first wedding while in Connecticut, in a little place called Danbury: Danbury, Connecticut.

And since then, I have sung for over 600 weddings and half that many funerals.

Hitchin' a Ride

I stayed at Windsor Locks until the war was over. By that time I was an acting Sergeant Major.

Uncle Sam offered me all kinds of benefits to stay in the Air Corps and work as a recruiter in New York City. I guess they thought I was a pretty good salesman or something. They offered me a commissioned officers rank of second lieutenant and the whole thing, but I turned it down. I was anxious to get home to my family and start the business up again.

I caught the first train from Hartford to Chicago.

Once I got to Chicago, I was told that the next train to Peoria wouldn't arrive for another 6 hours.

And even though I was carrying three overstuffed bags with me, I wasn't about to wait. First, I managed to catch a ride out to the highway. From there, I was able to bum a ride darn near all the way to Chillicothe.

I stuck my thumb out one more time and hitched another ride from Chillicothe to Peoria. I just couldn't wait to be home.

It was a cold day in January when I finally arrived home from the war.

And wow, was I happy to see everyone, Trudy and Michael, mom and dad, and even my brother Mitchell.

"Mitchell?" I thought. "What on earth are you doing here?" I was surprised to see him.

Well, unfortunately, he had gotten himself hurt in the spring of '45, and the Marines had shipped him home.

He'd already opened the business back up, but now that I was back home, he was ready to get out of it.

"All right the place is opened," he said. "I don't like it, I don't like the cleaning business; I'm going to go into the used car business. What do you want to do?"

He'd caught me completely off guard, "That's the only thing I know is the cleaning business."

"Well, do you want it?"

"What do you mean, do I want it?"

"Well, we'll become partners," he said. "And you'll run the business. I'm going to go into the used car business."

"Will you let me run it my way? The way I want to run it?"

"Yeah sure," he promised, "I won't interfere. Give me a few bucks out of it every week and it's yours."

Wow, let me tell you, I was in my glory. Here I was

fresh out of the Air Corps, home again with my family, and now I was being handed the keys to the family business. Life was good.

But it didn't take very long for me to come down off that cloud, because I soon realized that I'd been left in charge of a bunch of unpaid bills, literally thousands and thousands of dollars in unpaid bills.

Had I just jumped out of a plane without a parachute? What did I just get myself into?

So, I said, "Jim what are you going to do?"

Well, first of all, I started praying about it. And then, I rolled up my shirt sleeves and just started working my way through it, one day at a time.

Grape Shot out of a Cannon

When I first got out of the service, I felt like grape shot out of a cannon; there were a million different things to do and I was being pulled in a million different directions.

Priority one was the business. I went from rug repairman to rug-beater to pant presser in a hurry.

Not only did I press pants, but I was the regular repairman too. Heck, I couldn't afford a carpenter, an electrician, or a plumber, or any of those kinds of guys, so I had to learn to do it all on the fly.

We didn't have a gas fired boiler to create steam for the pressing machine or to dry the rugs in the dry room, we had a very old Kewanee boiler.

And once or twice a month new coal had to be added. The coal was dumped into a coal chute; from there the coal was fed into the fire by an auger.

Inevitably a couple times a month a big rock would get hooked up in this auger deal and the steam would go down. And there'd be ten or fifteen people sitting around not working while I'm down there trying to fix it, and it was absolute bedlam.

I should tell you, however, that the very first call I got was from my old friend Livy, Robert Livingston. He was now Father Livingston.

I wasn't surprised that he was a priest, but I was surprised that he was back in town.

And not only was he back in Peoria, but the Bishop made him choir director at St. Mary's Cathedral.

"Well," he told me, "now that you're home, you're singing in our choir."

"What? Wait a minute; I'm not even undressed yet. I've still got my uniform on."

"I don't give a dang, get down here! You're singing in our choir; we're singing together, down here at the cathedral."

And we did, for 23 years we sang together at St. Mary's Cathedral. And those were some of the happiest nights, some of the happiest occasions you could ever want.

Book 1: Chapter 30: Singing for a Beer

It seemed like I was working sixteen-hours six-days a week, and sometimes on Sunday too. However in between times, there was still this passion of mine called fast-pitch softball.

By the spring of '46, I had been asked to rejoin the team, and I didn't hesitate to say yes.

I was a few years older, but it was still good old fast-pitch softball, and Gipps Beer was still our sponsor.

I managed to play ball maybe once, sometimes two nights a week or on weekends and we traveled. Gipps provided us with buses and $3 dollars a day for food; you know, hamburgers, and things.

We traveled to Milwaukee, Des Moines, Rock Island, wherever. We were all over the Midwest. And we had really built a name for ourselves. Did I mention that we were State Champions three times?

On this version of the team, there were four of us that loved to sing, Tiny Neff, Mel Burdette, Don Jones, and myself.

Like I said, we traveled a lot, so we often found ourselves playing a game in some small community.

After the game, we always ended up at one of the local service clubs.

We'd buy our first beer, and then mingle around. Pretty soon all the ball players would be scattered throughout the room, and that's when we'd hit them with our first song.

Oh, we'd sing with all the gusto we could muster, and then afterwards, the people would just clap and clap and clap until someone bought a second beer for us, and the first thing you know, we had all the beer we could drink for the rest of night without paying anything for it.

During the week, when we played at home, down at Proctor Field, I could leave work at 6:30 p.m.; change clothes; go down and play ball; and come back home and work in my ball suit. That wasn't an unusual routine for me during the summer.

And on the weekends, after a home game, we would go down to the brewery right after the game and drink beer right out of the vats.

Lord have mercy, was that good?

A vat, you know, is huge, and these were, maybe four or five hundred gallon vats. And the guys from the brewery, from Gipps, would just open the spigot and let the beer come out.

Wow, that was the best beer in the world.

I golfed too in those days.

But when Gipps closed up in 1953, I spent more time on the greens.

One of my better employees at the cleaning plant was also one of the best golfers in the city of Peoria: a guy by the name of Russell Buchen – remember him, the dancer.

Russell and I, well, we'd have our golf clubs right in the work truck there, and every night at about 6:30 p.m., a quarter to 7 p.m., about ten or twelve of us would meet out at the Madison Golf course.

Fred Sprenger was a pro, he'd meet us over there, as would guys like Andy Paul and Roy MacIntyre.

These guys were some of the best golfers in the city. And I was learning. But being with good golfers like that you learn quick.

You learn, you better be able to hold your own, or they won't let you play anymore. But we used to play every night just about 'til dark and then get in the truck, go back to the cleaning plant, work 'til about 11 p.m. or 12 a.m., go to bed, and get up the next morning at six o'clock.

From '46 to '52, that was when I first became heavily involved in the community of Peoria.

Right after the war, Bob Lenhausen, Dave Connor, Dave Schlink, and a bunch of other veterans, we started sharing our experiences and stories with each other.

And I think it's fair to say, we were all a little taken back by what we heard outsiders saying about our hometown.

There were jokes about prostitutes lining up at city hall; Peoria was said to be a place where vice, gambling and graft flourished; and stories were retold about Peoria's sensational crime and political corruption. Peoria was the punch line of every foul-mouthed dirty joke we heard in the service. I mean, we were the laughingstock of cities all around the country.

And all of us who were in the service, we were the butt of those jokes.

We also knew that some of the jokes and some of the stories we heard weren't that far off target. Because, it was true, for example, that on every Saturday the prostitutes would line up near city hall to get their health examinations.

So, we decided we were going to change this somehow.

Most of us were former Jaycee's, so we already had

some knowledge of the community, and an interest in helping out, organizing, and making things better.

But it was going to take some time.

The Journal Star was still reporting sensational crimes, like when the president of one of the local railroads ended up being mysteriously killed in 1947.

And remember, in the mid-1940's, the Shelton gang was still running around Peoria trying to use their mafia tactics to control the local gambling. And that lasted until, what, at least 1948-'49, I believe.

By 1952 the city was about a million dollars in debt, mostly because of corruption – bad politics.

Honestly, this town needed a change. And our little group started working towards a city-manager form of government.

And one of the guys, who was very active in this group, was Bob Morgan. Now, Bob Morgan ended up being a federal judge.

But before he became a federal judge, he became the first mayor under the new form of government, a city-manager style of government. That was in 1953, and Peoria has operated under that system ever since.

Politics and community were already in my blood.

My Babies and My Business

I know how it might have sounded, but things weren't all bad here in Peoria.

In fact, there were a few good things beginning to happen simultaneously.

First of all, for us, Trudy gave birth to our second son, Mark, on July 23, 1949.

And by 1950, the business had paid off all its debts. Like another minor miracle, it only took four years to be debt free.

On October 11 of 1951, we celebrated the birth of our third son, Nick –named after my dad. And to top it off, October 11 of 1951 was also our son Michael's 9th birthday. How about that.

By 1952, Maloof Cleaners had 8 stores all over the city and Central Illinois.

Michael had become the bat boy for our softball team, and he would even travel with us a lot of the time.

Again, in 1953, the city-manager form of government was slowly beginning to restore our civic pride. And by the next year, Peoria was actually named an All-American City – the first of three times.

Gipps closed and fast-pitch softball came to an end.

I was still playing golf with Russell Buchen and those guys, I loved golf; I still love golf to this day.

And I also took up handball around this time.

There were about fifteen of us that would meet over at the YMCA, John Bearce, Hiles Stout, Mike Chianakas, and some others, and we'd play handball for an hour and a half or so, grab a shower, and then head back to work.

Also in 1953, the family moved from First Avenue. Trudy and I bought our first house; it was just off of Western Avenue, at 1922 W. Rohmann in West Peoria.

And on August 8, 1953, we were blessed with the arrival of our youngest child, our lovely daughter, Janice.

By 1955, Maloof Cleaners had expanded to eleven locations, and we were competing with Ideal Troy Cleaners for number one volume leader in the Peoria-area.

I think it is fair to say, I had my hands full. But I was young and full of energy, I thought sleep was overrated.

I even ended up with my own radio show called "Jimmy Maloof Sings." And that was in 1955-56. That was everyday at noon.

I'd run over from the cleaners during my lunch hour to sing.

And I was doing live television at WEEK, twice sometimes three times a week. They had a live show from 4-5 p.m. everyday, and I used to go over and sing.

And when I say "live" television, I mean live where if you goofed up, everybody knew about it. Heck, they saw it happen. They saw it, they laughed, and then called you later to laugh some more.

Sometimes, when I look back, even I don't know how I did it all, the singing, the softball, the golf, handball, the long hours at work, and now a family.

I don't know how I had time to make kids when I was as active as I was.

But, seriously though, my entire life, I've been a man on the go. It's always been that way. And I've loved every minute of it, you know, seize the day for tomorrow's promised to no man.

And, my wife, Trudy was a blessing from heaven, a real angel.

Through it all, she never stopped me. She didn't discourage me. She encouraged me. She was a fabulous mom, and she raised her four children beautifully. And as long as I was capable of doing what I was doing, she never complained. Never.

She truly was *The Wind Beneath My Wings*.

BOOK 2

The Memoirs of Jim Maloof

For every veteran, and I'm sure for many others too, the war was a landmark event. It became the language of our lives. Every event in your life, from that time forward would be referenced from that moment.

"I remember before the war, I did this..."

Or, "After the war, I did that..."

It was an event that would change your life forever, and after, you'd never be the same.

It wasn't exactly like you went home and picked up where you left off. It was almost like being born again, with every adventure new; and a thousand things to do; a "can do" attitude; and a renewed sense of pride.

I believe that more civic organizations were formed during this time than any other in the history of this country.

Book 2: Chapter 2: The Man with the Big Black Cigar

As for myself, after World War II, I took a renewed interest in my heritage and became heavily involved in the American Lebanese Syrian Society (ALSS).

I held several official positions within the ALSS during those years. I organized activities, eventually, became the club President a few times, and all that stuff. And as my involvement grew, one thing led to another, and I found myself involved in the Midwest Federation of Syrian Lebanese American Clubs.

And it was through the Midwest Federation that I met a charismatic, fiery, gentleman named Mike Tamer.

No matter where he went, he always had a big black cigar sticking out of his mouth. Sort of like George Burns, you never saw Mike Tamer without a cigar.

He was from Indianapolis. Like a lot of Lebanese, he was an entrepreneur (no surprise there). He was also a very successful entrepreneur, the owner of a tobacco and candy distributorship.

Tamer knew how to influence people, how to persuade people to do stuff, and no doubt, that's why he was elected President of the Midwest Federation.

He was a community leader; he loved to have fun; and was a real fireman, ready to go when the bell rang; a high-spirited guy, and full of enthusiasm, a real cheerleader.

We were somewhat alike, a couple of guys who

believed in our heritage; we liked to get things done; and we love helping people. We were both loud; enthusiastic; and could both be a bit crass. We were loyal; had big hearts; we loved to encourage people; and we loved to lead.

Little did I realize that my meeting Mike Tamer would set off a chain of events that would change my life. And boy did it ever.

The Call to Adventure

In the summer of 1957, I get a call from this guy named Haddad, Nimer Haddad. He said that Mike Tamer told him to call me.

"We've got this small group," he said, "that's meeting in Chicago. Danny Thomas wants to speak to us about a little project that he's got going. And we're calling on selected Lebanese-Syrian leaders from around the country that can come in and maybe help us get this project off the ground."

"Who else is going to this meeting?"

And he starts rattling off names like Tony Abraham and George Simon, and a bunch of guys like that.

Tony Abraham was the largest Chevrolet dealer in the city of Chicago for a number of years.

George Simon was an industrial parts giant out of Detroit. He was an incredibly successful businessman.

So, anyway, Haddad was dropping names like that, guys that were active in the Midwest Federation, and for the most part they were all millionaires.

And here I am, the lil' ol' pants presser from Peoria.

"What did they want with me?" I was wondering.

Honestly, I figured they wanted some kind of big money donation.

So, my first reaction was, "No. I don't have that kind of money. I've got a small business to run, and I've got a growing family. No, I can't do it."

"Don't worry about that Jim," Haddad said, "the guys in Chicago will take care of it. Listen, you and your wife are invited; we'll take care of dinner; you can stay over night on Saturday; go to church on Sunday morning; and then head back home afterwards. We'll take care of everything."

And I said, "No."

No, no, no, no!

I'm sure Tamer told him to call me, because this guy wouldn't take "no" for an answer, and that was Tamer's trademark.

So, I said, "Let me think about it."

Over dinner, I told Trudy about the call.

She asked me a bunch of questions, like, who was going to be there, when was it going to be, where would it be, and all that stuff.

Well, the meeting was actually going to be in early October, the month of my birthday.

Trudy suggested, "Why don't we take this as an opportunity for a little birthday trip to Chicago. We'll meet Danny Thomas, get a free hotel, free dinner, why not?"

I still thought I was getting the short end of the stick.

"Well, let me think about it," I told her.

About 4 or 5 days later, Haddad called back, twice.

And finally I said, "Okay, Mrs. Maloof says we'll come."

"Really?" Haddad said, like I had caught him off guard. "Okay, great. We have everybody else lined up. You were the last one, we were just waiting to hear from you. All right, we'll see you on Thursday."

"All right," I said, "we'll be there."

Book 2: Chapter 5: I Didn't Want To Go To Chicago

I was still hesitant about going to Chicago. I was suspicious of an entertainer wanting to head up some kind of little project that was probably going to be funded out of my pocket.

But Trudy could be very convincing when she wanted to be, and she wanted to be.

So, we showed up at the old Morrison Hotel, just like Trudy said we would.

The meeting was held in a private room, like a small banquet room, within the hotel. There were cocktails and little finger foods and whatnot on hand. We visited with Mike Tamer and some other people we knew.

We were told that Danny Thomas was still downstairs, he was just finishing up his early show.

We'd only been there short of an hour when Danny walked in the room.

Everybody that had been standing around talking now moved toward the door, towards Danny. Tamer and his wife, everybody just gravitated toward Danny. There were hand shakes and pats on the back and even a few hugs.

Trudy and I were sitting somewhere near the back of the room, and she looked at me and said, "Let's go, let's go."

I don't know why, but I said, "Un-uh, let's wait and see what happens."

And as Danny was shaking hands and talking with these other couples, somehow his eye caught mine.

He was looking across the room, as if he was looking right through those people. And as we made eye contact, he kind of nodded at me, as if to say, "I'm going to see you later," or something like that.

We'd just stood where we were at our table, and when he got done shaking hands with all of those people, then here he comes.

And his first words to me were, "So, you're Jim Maloof, the big shot from the cow town," or something like that.

I said, "Whoa, boy, we haven't even met yet. Don't be pulling that stuff."

We shook hands and then something strange happened. Like one of those minor miracles, or some kind of an inspired moment.

We stood there, in a firm handshake, and I was looking deep into his eyes, skeptically eyeing him up, and he back at me. And then all the sound in the room disappeared, and I saw deeper and deeper, it was as if I already knew him, as if we were some kind of long lost brothers.

And then he said, "I'm going to need you. Would you help me?"

"I-I don't know," I said, "I'm here because I want to help you, but I need to know more about you're little project."

He nodded and said, "We'll get to that very shortly."
I was now officially intrigued, but still skeptical.

As they sat us down to eat, I told Trudy, "Now, I really want to hear what this guy has to say."

Because all I really knew about Danny Thomas was that he was a big-time entertainer.

He'd started out on the radio; he was a comedian; he'd been in a few movies, including the *The Jazz Singer*, a few years back; and now had his own hit television show, *Make Room for Daddy*. I'd seen it, it was funny. Outside of that, I didn't know nothing.

A lot of guys, too many times, you'd hear about some guy in the entertainment business latching on to this cause or that, just to get his name out there. You know like a vehicle to up his reputation.

So, now I'm wondering, "What am I here for? And what's this guy's shtick?"

As we finished our meal, our host stood up and began telling us a bit about himself.

Like everybody else in room, he was Lebanese. His real name was Muzyad Yakhoob, but it got changed to Amos Jacobs, and his stage name, the name everybody knew him by was Danny Thomas.

He came from poor parents, immigrants; they lived upstairs over a bakery. His mom cleaned the pots and pans for the bakery, and in lieu of pay, she receive 4 or 5 loaves of bread a day for her seven kids.

"I come from a very small beginning, my parents are like your parents," he said. "And I would dare to say, most of your parents couldn't even read or write English when they came here."

Wow, that struck a note with me.

The more he talked, the more he said that was symbolic of what we had gone through, what our parents had gone through, and the more he talked the more I believed in what he had to say.

He wasn't talking about making a name for Danny Thomas. He was talking about giving back to the United States of America.

I don't know, he may have thought I was rich, but I wasn't, but in that room, there were some very wealthy people. People who had done well because Uncle Sam had opened the doors for their parents to come to this country, like himself; his parents had come to this country to enjoy the rights and freedoms and the whole thing.

"We have all done well," he said, "and we should not forget that. We should pay back."

I can just hear his words, "We should pay back for what this great country did for our parents, and how it gave all of us an opportunity to live as we are living, to do things. And I am here because I want you to help me do something."

He went back again and began telling us about the early years, during the depression; about how he was broke and penniless, out of work, and couldn't find a job as a Master of Ceremonies in Detroit.

All his life he wanted to be an emcee, but his wife wanted him to give up show business and get some job security, you know, get a job in a grocery store.

Not being able to give his family the security they wanted, not being able to fulfill his life ambition, Danny said he was feeling about as broke and hopeless as a guy could get. And then one day his life was changed, when someone told him about a forgotten saint, St. Jude Thaddeus, the Apostle, the patron saint of hopeless and impossible causes.

Down and out, he went to the Church of Saints Peter and Paul in Detroit, fell to his knees and prayed to St. Jude. "Help me find my place in life, and I'll build you a shrine," that was his promise.

And a short time later, he was offered a one week

stint as the Master of Ceremonies at the 5100 Club in Chicago. He became a hit, in fact, he was still working there three years later.

His life, however, hit another crossroads when he was offered equal-ownership of the 5100 Club, half the business. The only catch was that if he took the offer, he'd be the Master of Ceremonies at the 5100 Club, permanently.

"Do I take the job security?" he asked us, "or pursue my career?"

And even though he hadn't built the shrine yet, he once again turned to St. Jude. This time he prayed at St. Clement's Church in Chicago, and his prayer, "Show me the way. Give me just a small sign of what road I must take, and I'll dedicate my life to perpetuating your name."

And as St. Jude would have it, the head of the William Morris talent agency, Abe Lastfogel, happened to be in Chicago, happened to catch Danny's show and signed him to a contract.

His income more than doubled since working for the agency.

Now, he really owed St. Jude that shrine.

But somewhere along the way, he told us, he had found out that St. Jude already had a shrine, a national shrine in Chicago, it wasn't much, just a little side-alter in a church on the West Side. But it was there.

So now, Danny said, if he was going to build St. Jude a shrine, it was going to have to be better than that one.

For all of his success, he said, he never forgot his promise to St. Jude.

And one day, he decided to pay a visit to an old friend, Cardinal Stritch, the Roman Catholic Archbishop of Chicago.

The two had known each other since their days together in Toledo, when Danny had been Bishop Stritch's alter boy.

Immediately, upon the first visit, he started telling the cardinal his story, the story he was telling us. Except now, he was thinking of building a shrine with a statue.

And that's when the cardinal suggested instead of a shrine, what about a clinic.

"A clinic?" Danny said, "How am I going to afford a clinic?"

And that week, while he was pondering the cardinal's suggestion, he came across a story in the *Chicago Tribune*. And buried somewhere in the middle of the paper was a one-column story about 2" inches long.

It was about a young African-American boy down in Mississippi, who had been hit by a hit-and-run driver.

Some good Samaritan happened to see the boy lying by the curb. There was no one else around. He stopped, picked the youngster up, bundled him in a blanket, and rushed him to the nearest medical clinic.

"Can somebody help this boy, he's seriously hurt, he might die, can I get some help?"

They ask him, "Is this your child?"

"No, I found him lying on the street, down the road, can I get some help?"

"Well, we have to call his parents first, do you know his parents?"

"No. I don't know him at all. Look, I just found the kid."

"Well, how do we know if he has insurance? Who's going to pay the bill?"

And because the kid had no i.d. on him, the guy didn't know who his parents were or nothing like that, the clinic refused to help him.

So, the guy takes the kid, puts him back in his car, and speeds down the road looking for the nearest hospital or clinic.

A mile down the road, he finds a hospital.

He carries the kid in. Now the kid is weak and limp.

They put him on a stretcher.

And the man is telling them his story. "Look, I don't know this kid, I just found him on the side of the road. Can you help him?"

"You don't know who his parents are?"

"No, I don't know anything, but the kid's dying, can you help him?"

No i.d., no parents, the hospital would not help him.

And while they stood there and argued about it, the kid died, right there in the hospital, on a stretcher.

At first I was going to build a clinic, Danny said, a

little four bed shrine to St. Jude: a clinic where no child would ever be turned away for medical attention because of his family's inability to pay, or because his parents are out of work or have no insurance.

Any child that comes to this clinic, he said, is going to get free medical treatment.

And now, he said, unveiling a drawing, I've decided that the shrine will be a hospital for needy children, a place where they will be cared for regardless of race, religion or ability to pay - a hospital where no suffering child will be turned away.

Dr. Lemuel Diggs took the floor and began telling us about his work at the University of Tennessee.

Dr. Diggs worked in clinical pathology, and he was involved in the study of childhood diseases, namely leukemia and sickle cell anemia. "These are terminal diseases," he told us, "catastrophic diseases, diseases that are killing thousands and thousands of little children."

"There's a need for a hospital that can care for these children, and what we need is a research hospital devoted to the study of this type of illness. Studying this disease and doing the research is vital, because right now, only 4% of the children diagnosed with leukemia survive."

The drawing, now on an easel between the two men, was an aerial view of a building in the shape of a five-fingered star. Danny called it the "Star of Hope."

He said it was designed by a world famous, African-American, architect from Los Angeles named Paul Williams.

This was the hospital, Danny said, that he planned to build. It is to be a star of hope for all children who have catastrophic and incurable diseases.

"Don't worry about how this hospital is going to be paid for," Danny said, "that's not your concern. I'm raising the money, $2 million dollars, for the hospital, and you are not responsible for a dime of it. I'm not going to ask you for a dime for the construction of this hospital. That's my responsibility."

Danny Thomas, Abe Lastfogel, and a few others had already formed The St. Jude Hospital Foundation of California. It was this group that was collectively raising the $2 million dollars, along with the city of Memphis.

"However, earlier," Danny went on, "I talked about giving back. I talked about the Lebanese-Syrian community giving something back to this country for all that it has done for us and our parents.

"What I would like you to do, as members of the Lebanese-Syrian American families around the country is, I would like to have you help me raise the $300,000 dollars it will take to run the hospital's administration every year.

"I want to put together, here tonight, an organization called ALSAC, American Lebanese Syrian

Associated Charities, and that little acronym can also stand for Aiding Leukemia Stricken American Children. Anyway, I want to put together, here tonight, an organization called ALSAC, and it will be a tax-free corporation. But I need it to raise $300,000 dollars a year, every year.

"And let's face it, if it is successful, and let's pray it is, then your role will be to raise a little more money, every year, to keep the hospital open.

"And I want you to help me."

Oh, let me tell you, the room just erupted.

The reaction was so solid, so supportive. The room was charged with fevered emotion, clapping and whistling.

Everybody was saying, "Yes, we will do it." And, "Yes, we will help you."

"We will do whatever we can; whatever we need to do to raise the money, so no family will ever be turned away."

I mean, I can't even tell you what it was like, but maybe "amazing" would be one word; the other, "electric."

Little did I dream, I was becoming a part of medical history.

Bringing it Home

From Chicago, we all fanned out across the country, and went back from where we came. Danny wanted us, each and every one of us who were at that meeting, to take the message back home with us. To take the message to our individual clubs and ask them to help.

My home, of course, is Peoria, Illinois. And my club is the American Lebanese Syrian Society (the ALSS).

In Peoria we actually have two Lebanese clubs, the ALSS and the Itoo Society. I think the Lebanese-American population at that time was somewhere around five thousand.

So I called a friend of mine, Dan Deeb. Dan belonged to the Itoo Society. And I said, "Dan can you help me out?"

"I'll try," he said, "what's going on?"

So I told him the whole story, about what this country has done for our parents, about giving back, and about helping the children.

And finally, I said, "Dan, for some of the guys that were in that room that night, for some of them this is damn near pocket change. But I'm not a millionaire and I can't just cut a check and be done with it. But I want to do something. I want to do my part. I want to help."

"What are your plans?" Dan asked.

I said, "I'll call all the people in my club, but I

need you to call all the people in yours. We'll have one big meeting. And I'll talk to them about what Danny Thomas is trying to do."

"Okay," he said, "I'll help you. I don't know if they'll buy into the fact that you are trying to raise money for a hospital without being able to show anybody what it'll look like. And where did you say it's going to be?"

"In Memphis," I said. "But I don't know where."

"Somewhere in Memphis," Dan replied, sounding a little uncertain. "Right."

Book 2: Chapter 8: The Meeting

The meeting was held at the Itoo Club down on South Adams. There were about 75 to 80 people who attended.

I spoke to them about what Trudy and I had just witnessed. About how Danny told us what our role was, about paying back, and all that stuff.

And I told them how Danny was now asking us, as Lebanese-Syrians across the country, to join him in raising $300,000 dollars a year – so no child would be left behind.

"I don't want your money tonight," I told them. "What I'd like you to do tonight is make a pledge. I'd like to have you pledge, either a 3 year pledge or a 5 year pledge, saying I will give you 'x' amount of dollars a year for 3 or 5 years."

At that first meeting, we had some of the more prominent Lebanese families in Peoria attend, the Couri's, the Rashid's, the LaHood's, the Joseph's, and, yes, the Maloof's. We had people from all walks in the community make pledges that night. Most of them made pledges for $100 dollars for 5 years.

Book 2: Chapter 9: The Totals Please

Within a week of that first meeting, when we knew how much they had pledged, and I called Mike Tamer with the totals.

Tamer was now Danny's go-to guy; officially he was the National Executive Director of ALSAC (American Lebanese Syrian Associated Charities). And there couldn't have been a better gentleman for the job either.

Tamer put Danny on the phone, and so, I told him the numbers too.

"How did you raise that money?" he said.

And I told him.

"I don't believe it," Danny cried out. "You raised that money in Peoria? Nobody even knows where Peoria's at."

I said, "Boy, you will, sooner or later, you will."

And in all, we raised $8,000 dollars that night: eight thousand from that first meeting.

And Danny was absolutely thrilled. Not because of the money number, but because the people of our heritage were buying into this "dream" of his; and that's what really made him happy.

The First Big Little Steps

The following year, in 1958, ALSAC held its first national convention. Just to reiterate here for a second, ALSAC was created with the sole intent and purpose of being the fundraising arm of St. Jude Children's Research Hospital {not yet built}.

ALSAC was comprised of people who were of Lebanese-Syrian decent. And it was our job to raise the money to pay for the day-to-day operations of the hospital {when it opened}.

And so, now it's 1958, and we are in Chicago at the first national convention and Mike Tamer asks me, of all people, to sing a song.

I chose "The Impossible Dream."

Since then, I can't tell you how many times that song has been sung over the years at St. Jude events. "The Impossible Dream" became the unofficial theme song for Danny Thomas and St. Jude.

What an honor that was. What an honor.

I was also elected to the ALSAC Board of Directors at that meeting, another honor.

And because of my appointment, I was privileged to meet some of the early movers and shakers. Of course, I had already met Danny Thomas, and I already knew Mike Tamer.

And now I got to know people like Ed Barry and

Fred Gattas, Sr. I mean I'd met them before, but now I got to know them on a personal level.

Ed was a lawyer from Memphis. He was very civic minded, a philanthropist; and twice already, he had raised large sums of money to start new hospitals, in Memphis.

Ed bought into the project right away and was the key in getting the Mayor and other leaders of Memphis, as well as the community, on board.

People in Memphis were raising money for this "dream" too.

And Fred Gattas, Sr., was a big catalogue publisher from Tennessee; and he was Lebanese. He spearheaded the first big Lebanese-Syrian fundraiser back in 1955. I think he raised somewhere around $5,000 dollars with that initial effort.

I must admit, it was very exciting to hear what these other guys were doing, or had done, and it just set the bar higher, and made me more determined to raise more money.

And so, in that year of 1958, Dan and I, we worked a little harder and thought a little bigger. We took the message to the larger community of Peoria through a letter campaign and personal appearances. And we also put together a little committee to keep things organized.

I was worried about what the final tally might be, because in 1958 in Peoria, it was a tough year. Caterpillar went on strike, as did the *Journal Star*. There were industrial lay-offs, and all this, you know, it didn't help the economy any.

When we received the totals from the second pledge drive, we were happy to find that we had raised $11,000 dollars.

And when I called my numbers in to Mike Tamer, he reacted just as before, "I don't believe it," he said, "I just don't believe it."

Around 150 chapters across the nation had now been formed, and in terms of numbers, Peoria was right there near the top of the list.

And Danny, when he heard this, thought it was unbelievable that "this little cow town called Peoria" could raise that kind of money, with no blueprint, no line drawing, nothing.

And I told him, I said, "Danny, if I can get you to come to Peoria, we'll get you bigger numbers."

And just like that, Mike Tamer arranged it, and Danny Thomas said he'd be here in June.

On November 2, 1958, there was a ground breaking ceremony in Memphis, Tennessee. A seventeen-acre site had been chosen for the home of St. Jude Children's Research Hospital. It was to be located adjacent to St. Joseph's Hospital.

And the first research staff was hired, they would work out of the University of Tennessee until the hospital was built.

This was all very exciting news: tangible evidence, that if you believe, you shall receive.

What About the Fieldhouse?

Danny's coming! Danny's coming!

The first obstacle we had to overcome was finding a place to host the event.

The news created quite a stir here in our little community. I mean, Danny Thomas was kind of a big deal. He had done a USO tour with Marlene Dietrich. He had starred on the big screen opposite Doris Day; he was an Emmy winning actor, and the star of an Emmy winning television show.

You have to remember, there was no Peoria Civic Center back in 1959. And we were also thinking, the space has to be big enough so that we can have a variety show.

Of course, immediately, I thought, "What about the Bradley Fieldhouse?" Bradley was a popular place. B.U. fever was running high, the men's basketball team had been to the final four in '54, and had just won the N.I.T. in '57, and it looked like they were primed for another run. And I've got to say, I was a fan.

So, anyway, I went to Bradley University and told them the deal.

They said, "No."

"Well, why not?"

They said that the Fieldhouse was strictly for Bradley affairs.

I didn't like that too much, but, what are you going

to do? I was moving on to plan two.

Then, and I don't know whose idea it was, but somebody came up to me and said, "Well, if that's the way Bradley wants it, then why don't you make Bradley a co-sponsor of the event, and call it something like 'An evening with Danny Thomas at the Bradley Fieldhouse.'"

"Bingo." That was it.

So, I talked to one of the men's clubs over there, and they agreed to co-sponsor the event.

Book 2: Chapter 12: **Life was Passing by Rather Fast**

In 1959, Mike Tamer had become the official fundraising head of ALSAC. And he made me a regional director for ALSAC. So, what did that mean? It meant that now I was in charge of raising funds in 6 Midwestern states.

No question, I was busier than ever before. I had more obligations, but hadn't given any up yet either. Honestly, life was passing by rather fast.

Our oldest boy, Michael, was heading into his senior year; while our youngest, our daughter Janice, was just out of kindergarten.

And now, it's June. I've got Danny Thomas arriving in Peoria on Friday, and we've got the show at the Bradley Fieldhouse on Saturday night.

And a friend of mine from over at WMBD-TV, the local CBS affiliate here in Peoria, had told me, "if you can get Danny over here on Friday night, after the 10 o'clock news, we'll put him on live."

"Okay, we'll see," I told him. And I'm thinking, "Like I don't already have a million things going through my mind."

And then on Wednesday, June 3, my dad died.

Funeral services were set for Saturday morning.

In those days, they called it "a hardening of the arteries," today it's called Alzheimer's Disease.

I was heartbroken. My dad had been a rock for this family. He had provided for us, been an example for us. He started the company I was now running. In fact, he only retired from the family business the year before.

I told the whole family that I was going to withdraw from the weekend's activities. I mean, I didn't really feel like doing it under these circumstances. I thought I'd let Dan Deeb or somebody else take over. But my mother kept saying, "No. You gotta do what you're supposed to do. Your dad would want you to do this."

In the end, mom's always right, that why she's mom. But out of what I felt was a courtesy to my dad, I wore a black armband that whole week, at the banquet, at the show, wherever I went I wore that black armband as a tribute to my dad.

N. Maloof, 77, Cleaning Firm Founder Dies

Obituary from the Peoria Journal Star, Thursday, June 4, 1959, Section A-16, Evening Edition –

Nimer Maloof, 77, a resident of 401 W. First Avenue, for 48 years and founder of the Maloof Cleaners here died at 4 p.m. Wednesday (June 3) at St. Francis Hospital where he had been a patient since March 30.

Born in Zahle, Lebanon, in February, 1882, he was a son of Abraham and Raghe Maloof. He married Sarah Zyne at New York City in November 1907 and they came to Peoria 51 years ago. He founded the cleaning establishment that bears his name at that time and operated it for a half a century, retiring a year ago. He was a member of St. Mary's Cathedral, the American Lebanese Syrian Society, and Spalding Council, Knights of Columbus.

Surviving are his fours sons, Mitchell J. Maloof and James A. Maloof, both of Peoria. Abraham J. Maloof of Indianapolis, Ind., And Maj. Fred M. Maloof of Washington D.C., one brother Sam Maloof of Peoria: 14 grandchildren and one great grandchild.

Funeral services will be at 8:15 a.m. Saturday at the Wilton Mortuary, 2101 N. Knoxville Avenue and at 8:45 at St. Mary's Cathedral. Msgr. Murray V. Hass will officiate. Burial will be in the St. Joseph's Cemetery.

Friends may call the mortuary at 3 p.m. Friday. The Rosary will be recited there at 8 p.m.

Memorial contributions may be sent to the St. Jude Hospital Fund.

Danny's Arrival

So, now Danny arrives in Peoria. He had traveled 32 cities in 28 days. He was absolutely exhausted.

He was just completely bombed out. He was so tired that the first thing we did when he hit town was we took him right up to St. Francis Hospital where he got a shot of B12 vitamins. I don't know, it was supposed to give him some more energy, or something - he still had 2 more cities left to go, the poor guy.

The itinerary for Danny was pretty simple:
Friday afternoon – A visit to St. Joseph's Home
Friday night – A banquet in honor of Danny
Saturday afternoon – A visit to the Peoria State Hospital
Saturday evening – St. Jude Fundraiser at the Bradley Fieldhouse.

Now it was Danny who wanted to go to St. Joseph's Home. It was a retirement home out on Heading Avenue.

And the reason he wanted to go is because St. Joseph's is designed like a star: literally darn near like the Star of Hope that Paul Williams had planned to build for St. Jude.

And Danny was very anxious to see what it looked like from the inside.

So after we took him to the hospital and got him some food, we drove him over to the home.

Book 2: Chapter 14: The Show Must Go On

That evening there was a big banquet at the Père Marquette held in Danny Thomas's honor. There were hundreds of people there, mostly from the Lebanese community, who had turned out to meet the star.

And as we were sitting at one of the banquet tables, Danny leans over and says to me, "How are tickets going for the show tomorrow night?"

I was a little bit embarrassed to say, "We only have about 2,100 or 2,200 tickets sold."

"Oh, we can do better than that," he said.

I didn't know what to say, I felt kind of foolish. But before I had to say anything in reply, I remembered the WMBD offer.

"Well," I said, "I've got a deal for you."

"What's that?"

"I've got a friend over at WMBD Radio and Television; it's only about a block away; and he said, 'if I can get you over to the station, after the ten o'clock news...'"

"Are you kidding?" Danny said.

"No. In fact, he said you can talk as long as you want."

"Well, what are we sitting here for? Let's do it."

So about 10:25 p.m. we graciously excused ourselves and started walking over to the old Orpheum Theater where WMBD had their studio set up.

We walked in and saw Jim Jenson, who was the host at the time. We explained the situation to him, and he said, "Sure, let's do this."

They quickly set up some chairs, where Jenson could do the interview.

"In just a minute, we'll stop the movie," somebody from master control said to Jenson.

Back in those days, they used to have movies at ten thirty, and, so, this night, they voluntarily stopped the movie to host a live interview with Danny Thomas.

Jenson interviewed him for a good hour and twenty minutes.

And Danny, with all of his God-given charm, began telling the television audience the same wonderful stories I had heard only a few years earlier at the Morrison Hotel in Chicago.

I got chills all over again.

The next morning, Saturday morning, I get an early call from Mike Tamer.

He wants to go over Danny's schedule.

I tell him that I'm planning on taking Danny over to the Peoria State Hospital in Bartonville.

About a week before Danny's arrival, I had received a phone call from a Dr. Klein.

Now, Dr. Klein was the Medical Director at the Peoria State Hospital, and I knew him rather well, because on occasion, I would go over to the hospital and sing for the patients.

So, Dr. Klein calls and says, "Hey Jim, I understand you have Danny Thomas coming to Peoria?"

"Yeah," I said, you know, thinking, "Okay what does this guy want?"

"Please, Jim," he said, "don't say 'no' to me. If you could just get him down here to say 'hello' to the patients, it would be . . . well, they would just love it. They listen to him on the radio all the time. They love him Jim. They just love him. It would be the best medicine you could provide for these people who are in so much need."

And, so, I tell Tamer all of this, and I also tell him, that's where we're going to be this afternoon.

"Whatever you do, Jim," he warned me, "you can't do that. You can't do that, he'll never go. He'll never go."

"But Mike, you told me that if Danny Thomas came to Peoria, he's mine, and I can do with him whatever I want? Wasn't that the deal?"

I thought Tamer was going to go nuts. He had a fit, he was so against it.

But finally he said, "Okay, but just don't tell him where you're taking him, because if you do, he won't go. He won't go to where the mentally disturbed people are."

Oh boy! I hung up the phone thinking, "Now what do I do?"

Book 2: Chapter 16: **Late Morning Coffee**

I met the guys for a late breakfast at the coffee shop inside the Hotel Père Marquette. Danny was there and so was George Shadid.

George was a policeman assigned to being Danny's chauffer and personal body guard while Danny was in town.

So, there were the three of us and a couple of other friends showed up too.

We are all sitting there having our coffee when Danny says, "Well, where are we going this morning? I want to get myself in the mind set to properly address the people we'll be talking to today."

I had called the other guys earlier and told them not to say a word. "I'll handle it," I'd told them.

Now, I didn't know what to do. So, I changed the subject. I started talking about the show tonight, what the Fieldhouse was like inside, how it was decorated, whatever I could think of.

Now it was about 11:20 a.m. and time to get into the car – it was some kind of big limousine. We began by giving Danny the grand tour of the downtown, and then we start heading over towards Bartonville.

Since there's a lot of junk yards and stuff on the way out of town, I imagine Danny was starting to get a little curious.

And as we got into Bartonville, he said, "Where are we going?"

I tried to change the subject, again.

And he asked again, "Where are we going?"

I just kept talking to the other guys in the back seat and wouldn't respond to him.

And as we were turning up Garfield hill to go to the hospital, Danny said, "Stop this car! Stop it."

We thought something was really wrong.

But, no, he turns around and says, "Now #!@$% it!" He could really cuss when he got all excited. (A little known fact, but Danny Thomas was a real pro at cussing.) So to paraphrase, he said, "This car's not going another two feet until I know where we're going."

I caved in and said, "All right! All right! I'll tell you where we're going." And I told him why I hadn't told him.

"You dumb S.O.B., don't you know," he said. "Don't you know that I have entertained shell-shocked American troops all over Europe; all over the world; I know what these mentally deranged people are like. They need our help more than anybody."

"No, I don't. I'm only following orders," I stammered.

"I want to be there," he said, "Those people need as much help, or more, than the kids we are trying to help."

And so, bless him, he said, "Get on it George. Let's get up this hill and go see these people."

Well, it's 90 degrees out, hot and humid, as we drive up to the Peoria State Hospital.

All the arrangements had been made for the families and patients to be outside; and there must have been 800 people gathered all around the softball diamond.

Their cars were parked all over the infield and outfield.

There were patients sitting in a semi-circle in their wheelchairs, just waiting for Danny Thomas to arrive.

To add to the excitement, the cars were all honking their horns, the noon whistle was going off, and people were clapping.

As I was trying to introduce Dr. Klein to Danny, I was literally yelling. I could hardly hear myself speak for all the hallelujah going on.

And in spite of all that, above all of the dither and excitement, above all the pandemonium that was happening, came the pleas and the cry of a small boy's voice.

Above all of that noise, you could hear that youngster from about 50 feet away.

"Danny, Danny, I've got to see Danny!" He was screaming as if he was hurt. It was such a strong appeal.

Finally Danny said, "Excuse me Dr. Klein, where

"My life was transformed from the moment I first met Danny Thomas."

Jim Maloof and Danny Thomas met for the first time in October of 1957 at
the old **Morrison Hotel** in downtown Chicago as seen in this postcard circa 1930.
Built in 1925 and over 40 floors high, this historic building was demolished in 1965.

"The Lion" Mike Tamer

above: *(c)* **Mike Tamer** at the unveiling of his portrait. *(r)* A rare shot of **Danny Thomas** wearing his glasses.
below: **Mike Tamer**, **Jim Maloof**, and **Danny Thomas** at an early American Lebanese Syrian Associated Charities (ALSAC) meeting.

above: **Marge Crowl**: a key to the success of what eventually became the Teen March

below: Getting ready to hang posters announcing the "**Teenagers March**."

Barbara Higgins, Julie Downs, Carol Harnickle, and Connie Syner.

above: **Danny Thomas** with **Tim Gura, Mary Slevin, Mark Maloof,** and **Jim Maloof.**

below: In this picture you can see the first Teen March collection canister.

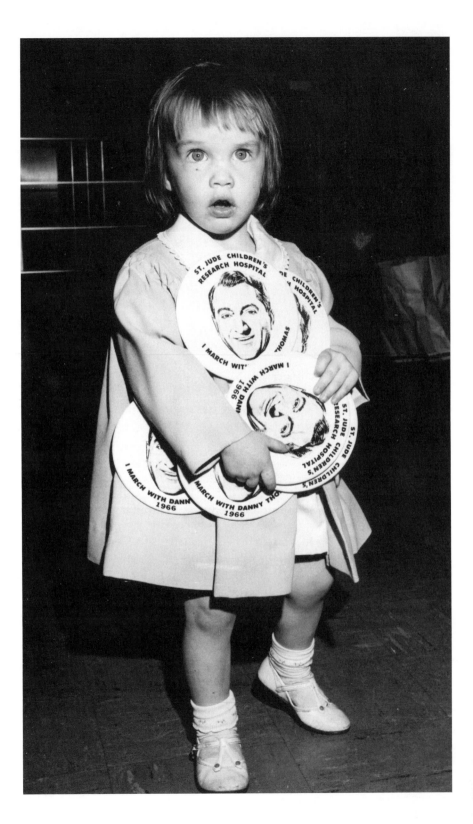

above: **Trudy Maloof** at a Teen March Banquet.
below: A large group of Teen Marchers gather outside of McDonald's
on Western and Rohmann, Peoria, Illinois. (1961).

far left: **Danny Thom**
unveils the 10-foot wh
marble statue of St. Ju
during the formal opening
St. Jude Children's Resear
Hospital in Memph
Tennessee, on Feb. 4, 196

left The statue of **St. Ju**
Thaddeus, the patron sai
of hopeless and lost cause

above: **Danny Thomas** is second from left on the opposite page. **Jim Maloof** -on the far right of this page- is seen here talking to **Fred Gattas**.

right: **Ed Barry** and **Danny Thomas.** In the earliest days of St. Jude, Ed Barry paid the staff out of his own pocket when there was no money to continue.

above: **Jim Maloof** sings "Bless This House."

below: **Jim Maloof** claps to a speech given supporting St. Jude.

above: Twice **Jim** was asked to sing professionally: once by Horace Heidt, and another time by Abe Lastfogel, the owner of the William Morris Agency in Los Angeles.

♫ ♪ ♫ ♪ ♫ ♪ ♫ ♪ ♫ ♪

A few of the
Sisters
of **Epsilon
Sigma Alpha,**
a non-
collegiate
sorority
with more
than 30,000
members.

In 40 years of service to St. Jude Children's Research Hospital, **ESA** has raised in excess of $160 million dollars.

above: **Jim and Trudy Maloof** head off to their son's football ballgame.

below: (l) **Jim**, always the tireless campaigner, takes a well deserved nap (1961).

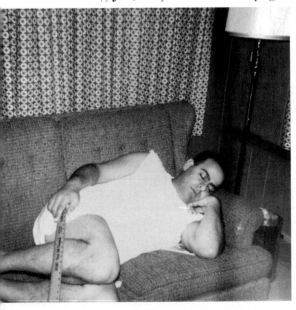

above: Time for friends

Pat O'Brien

above: **Jim** visits with actor **Pat O'Brien.** O'Brien played opposite Ronald Reagan in the 1940 movie *Knute Rockne, All American.* It was O'Brien's title character who said, *'Let's win one for the Gipper!'*

right: **"Anything for a Laugh" Maloof** performs in one of the many skits he's acted in at St. Jude functions.

right: Inside the brand new **Ramada Inn Hotel** here in Peoria. The banquet hall is ready for Danny's visit (1966).
insert: **Roy Demanes**

below Before he was the Founder of St. Jude Children's Reseach Hospital, **Danny Thomas** was a comedian. Here Danny is seen clowning around for the camera.

above: My brother **Mitchell Maloof** *(third from left)* and his wife **Delores** *(far right)*

below: A very early **Jim Maloof Realty** sign, circa 1970.

Dancing with Danny's sister

is that voice coming from? Take me to that voice."

We saw a nurse who pointed down to a young lad in a wheelchair.

Danny said, "Take me to that kid."

So, Danny walked over, we all walked over, and Danny knelt down in front of this youngster.

And the nurse, being very astute, pointed to his eyes, as if to say he was blind.

He could not see. He was palsied and blind, and trembling so hard.

The young man had clutched in his hand a white envelope. And he was so excited at the moment that he just couldn't hold himself back. He kept screaming, "Danny, Danny, I've got to see Danny."

And Danny said, "Hi. Hi, I'm Danny Thomas."

"You're Danny Thomas?" an unbelieving voice ushered back.

Danny took the boy's hand and put it on his cheek, on Danny's cheek, to give the young boy some assurance.

"Are you really Danny Thomas?"

"Yes. Yes." And Danny held his hand and gave him a hug.

And the kid was crying out, not out of desperation, but out of excitement, and he said, "When I heard you were coming to visit us here at the hospital, I started saving my candy and gum money."

In his palsied little hand, he clutched the little white envelope, and it shook as he spoke. "I want to give this to you, now, so that you can go help the children that you are trying to cure."

"What's in the envelope?"

"It's 75 cents, and it's all yours Danny Thomas."

And, Oh my gracious! I've been around a few years here and there, and I've seen adults, grown people cry, but Danny broke up. He sobbed. It took a minute or more for him to pull himself together.

He just sobbed and cried as this beautiful young man introduced himself, "M-m-my n-name is B-B-Billy J-Johnson. I'm eleven years-old, and I've been saving my money for you."

When Danny finally pulled himself together, he looked up and cried out, "My God. My God, help us. Here's a young man who needs more help than any of those we are trying to serve, and he's saving his money to help this cause."

Then he lifted the kid up out of the wheelchair and walked him over, about 100 feet away, out to the pitcher's mound, right there in the heart of the field.

And out there on the diamond was my friend, Gene Farris, playing "Danny Boy" on the piano.

With tears in his eyes, Danny said, "Go sing a song, Jim."

He caught me off guard, and I said, "Wait a minute, this is your show."

"Sing a song," he told me, "now."

"What do you want me to sing?"

"I don't know, just get out there and sing. I need a minute to pull myself together."

So, without thinking about it, I just started singing

How Great Thou Art.

> *O Lord my God,*
> *When I in awesome wonder*
> *Consider all*
> *The works Thy Hand hath made*
> *I see the stars,*
> *I hear the mighty thunder,*
> *Thy pow'r throughout*
> *The universe displayed*

And after singing the first verse, I asked the parents and the patients to sing along, and everybody sang along with me.

> *Then sings my soul,*
> *My Savior God, to Thee,*
> *How Great Thou Art!*
> *How Great Thou Art!*

After the song, I introduced Danny. And he vowed to everybody sitting there and standing there, to everyone in attendance, that one day this little white envelope, which had Billy Johnson's seventy-five cents in it, would be placed in the cornerstone of the St. Jude statue at the St. Jude Children's Research Hospital in Memphis, Tennessee.

The Benefit at the Fieldhouse

There was no question that God was doing wonderful and miraculous things here in Peoria.

And if there had been any doubt, well, Billy Johnson erased it all. The events of the afternoon were all we could talk about, but we still had a fundraiser at the Fieldhouse ahead of us.

The thought of so many empty seats filled the pit of my stomach. The Fieldhouse seats about 7,300 people, and as of the night before, if you recall, we only had 2,100 or 2,200 tickets sold.

By 6:00 p.m. we were doing soundchecks, getting our show clothes on, and going over all the last minute details. And I have to tell you, I still wasn't feeling too good.

The people showed up slowly, slowly. Every time I'd peek out the curtain, there'd be a few more faces in the audience; a few more faces in the audience.

But by the time the curtain opened, there were a lot more people out there. I don't know where they came from, but I was happy they were there.

I opened up with a song accompanied by my good friend Gene Farris and a large orchestra, which he had assembled.

Then another good friend, Mike Dentino came out and did a hilarious stand-up comedy routine that he had written especially for the occasion.

We also had a young 18-year old gymnast by the name of Theresa Montafusco on hand. She performed a wonderful acrobatic routine for us, and I believe by this time, she had already won herself a place on the 1960 U.S. Women's Olympic team. So, anyway, we were very excited to have her on hand, and she was also a native Peorian: and Italian, like Dentino.

And then, of course, I came out and sang just a little more.

But the thing I remember most about that night was that by the time Danny Thomas took the stage, he was looking out on 7,200 faces.

Now where did those 5,000 people come from?

I'm sure that most of those people had seen Danny Thomas on WMBD-TV the night before. But 5,000 additional people, in the course of twenty-four hours, had made a decision to support this "dream" of Danny Thomas's, you can say what you like, but to me it was a minor miracle.

Overall that year, we raised just over $22,000 dollars. That's pretty good considering the average worker in Peoria made less than $5,000 dollars a year, and the cost of a house in 1959 was somewhere around $12,000 dollars.

Twenty-two thousand dollars was looking pretty good.

The Mother's March

Now the notoriety, or popularity, of St. Jude was really picking up across the country, and certainly here in Peoria.

Every year, we just continued to raise more and more money.

And because we'd done such a good job, now it was time to really start thinking about boot money.

Anyway, I suggested that we have a Mother's March for St. Jude. Mother's going door-to-door was very popular at that time.

I started to put together a small group, but we needed a chairperson.

The big question was who could I get to head it?

I remember someone saying to me, "Marge Crowl! She's a workaholic. If you can get Marge Crowl to take over the chairmanship of your march, you'll have a good chance of it being a success."

"Do I know her?"

"Maybe not. She's not a big name in the community, but she is a worker. She's never been married. She's a telephone operator at Keystone, and attends St. John's Church down on the South Side, if that helps at all."

"Don't ring a bell, but I'd sure like to meet her."

And so, I went down to visit her, and she liked what I had to say. "I'm ready to help," she said.

"Wow. Lord have mercy!"

"I'll do whatever I can to help. It sounds like a great cause."

She began gathering mothers all over the city, and broke the city up into districts. You know, she really started to get this thing organized.

But we were running into some obstacles.

The main one was that we didn't have a lot of lee-time, it was about six weeks out from the proposed date of the march. And for whatever reason, we weren't getting as many mothers to sign up as we thought.

Now it was about a week before the first Saturday in May; that was going to be the day of the march; and we only had about thirty women recruited to go door-to-door throughout the whole central Illinois area, and that didn't bode well for a good drive.

You just can't run a drive with that few women. So, I thought, "How about high school kids?"

I knew at Spalding Institute there was a young man by the name of Tim Gura.

Tim and our son Mark had grown-up together at Saint Mark Catholic School. And our families knew each other from St. Mark's Church.

Tim was quite the leader.

He wasn't an athlete, but a leader; he just knew that everyone looked to him to get things done. You could here it in the way he spoke, and see it through what he accomplished. As only a sophomore, he was already president of the student council.

So, I called Tim on a Monday, six days before the drive, and asked him, "Could you please stop by after school tonight."

After school he stopped over to the house. And I began to explain the whole thing to him.

"What do you want from me," he asked.

"Tim," I said, "we need teenagers. We need as many teenagers as we can get between now and say Friday, to assemble them on Saturday, and go door-to-door collecting money for St. Jude."

While Tim Gura was trying to round up some teenagers, I went to see Tom Liston, president of P.A. Bergner & Co., to ask for one hundred shopping bags.

"What do you need the bags for?"

"We just need some bags that we can put the Mother's March supplies in." There was a long pause.

"Tom, am I asking for too much? I just need some sturdy bags."

Next stop, I went over and visited with Ed Peters. Ed was the station manager over at WMBD.

Ed was also a part of our Mother's March team. He was part of the brain trust that was in charge of creating the on-air promos and that kind of stuff.

He said, "We are going to ask for money. But, if we are going to ask for money, we're going to have to tell people how much to give."

"You can't do that," I said. "You must be crazy, you can't tell people what to give. Just say, 'Give.'"

"Yes," Ed said, "we can."

On Tuesday night, Richard Unes and Ed both came by the house to brainstorm. Ed and I filled Richard in on the change from "Mother's March" to "Teen March." Then, after we had gone through a bottle of Chivas Regal, Ed finally said, "Here's our slogan, 'When you see a teen at your door with a Danny Thomas button on, give a dollar.'"

I said, "No."

"Jim," he said, "I'm in the marketing business. Would you just listen to me."

WMBD promoted it on air Wednesday, Thursday, and Friday.

Well, Friday came around and what do you think happened?

I kid you not, Tim Gura had signed up nearly 400 high schoolers from all over, not only Peoria, but from Morton, Washington, Pekin, and East Peoria. Wherever he could recruit them from, he got them.

And while this sophomore in high school is recruiting an army of 400, it was like pulling teeth to get Tom Liston over there at Bergner's to give me some 5 cent shopping bags. But he did, after a week of begging, Tom finally gave us one hundred shopping bags to haul our supplies around in.

And then, on Saturday, I don't know how Marge Crowl assembled them, but she sent them all out to different areas of the city that morning: one mother leading ten-to-twelve teenagers.

I think it was after 3 p.m. when they all came back.

On Sunday, they assembled at the South Side Bank, down on South Adams Street, and brought their monies in to be counted. It was amazing, those 30 mothers and 400 teenagers raised $26,000 dollars.

And as God would have it, Ed Peters was right: close to twenty-two thousand of it was in greenback.

Ed was absolutely right.

Book 2: Chapter 22: Construction Begins

In 1960 construction started on St. Jude
Children's Research Hospital in Memphis, and Ed Barry
became the first Chairman of the St. Jude Board.

There was definitely an excitement in the air that
year.

Our "Teen March" had been a miraculous success.
And, wow, it planted a seed. Danny and Mike Tamer fell
in love with the idea of Teen Marches. Wherever Danny
went around the country, he talked about "Healthy Kids
Helping Sick Kids."

And he beat that drum like a song, he recruited
thousands and thousands of young people all across the
country to do the same thing we did here.

The next year, Bloomington, Illinois, started
a "Teen March." And our committee had a lot more
organizational help, and teens stepping up to be team
leaders.

We raised $40,000 in 1961.

The "Teen March" made millions and millions of
dollars for St. Jude until about twenty years ago (late
1980's – early 1990's). I guess the authorities and the
management people at St. Jude (in Memphis) thought
it got to be kind of risky having kids go door-to-door
asking for money, thinking some little girl might get into
problems with some goofy guy or something.

But over the years, the nationwide "Teen March" raised a lot of money to do a lot of good for a lot of hurting families.

It should be noted that also in 1961, the St. Jude Board of Governors along with a search committee finally hired a medical director for St. Jude Children's Hospital, his name Dr. Donald Pinkel.

Dr. Pinkel was the former head of pediatrics at Roswell Park Memorial Institute in Buffalo, New York. It was going to be his job to oversee the day-to-day operations of the hospital.

Book 2: Chapter 23: The Day Before

And so the dedication of St. Jude Children's
Research Hospital was set for Sunday, February, 4, 1962
at 2 p.m.

The night before the dedication of the hospital
there was a banquet, a big party, honoring Ed Barry for
all that he'd done.

So everybody that would be at the dedication, or at
least all of the core people, would also be at the banquet,
which meant that we were down in Memphis a day
earlier.

Anyway, Trudy and I are sitting down in the lobby
of the world's first Holiday Inn, which was in Memphis,
when out of the elevator pops Danny and his wife Rose
Marie, and with them a cameraman, still rolling I guess.

"Hey, Jim! Rosie and I are going to get a preview
of the hospital before the big crowd shows up tomorrow.
Why don't you and Trudy come along with us?"

"Oh sure, we'd be glad to."

So, we go out, get in the car, and head over.

As the car pulls up to the hospital, we see four
nuns standing by the curb, very excited and very
animated. They're waving and yelling our way.

"Now, these aren't just any nuns," Danny said
pointing out the window. "These are the Franciscan
nuns selected to be in charge of the hospital's
administration. They are going to run the place."

And with that, we got out of the car. The Sisters were all a quiver saying, "Oh, we have a big surprise for you."

But Danny stopped them, "Wait a minute, save some of that for tomorrow. We're going to go see the hospital right now."

That seemed to appease them, and they agreed to give us a grand tour of the place.

They took us all over. On the first floor were the treatment rooms. On the second floor the administrative offices. We saw everything you could possibly want to see.

Just as we were finishing our tour, I finally said, "I can't believe there's no chapel in here?"

In the original design, somehow, a chapel had been overlooked, and there was no place to put one either.

"Yes," they said looking at Danny, "remember we've been telling you that we had to have a chapel?"

While we were talking, they lead us down a dead-end corridor. Then they paused in front of a door and stopped talking, they became dead silent.

The head nun pulled her keys out; opened the door; and gestured for us to walk in.

"Oh, my God," Danny exclaimed. "What is this!"

"Just leave it to us, Danny," the nuns said. "We know how to work with these people and these contractors. We usually get what we want: after all, we are doing God's work."

It was beautiful. It was an all-faith chapel, for Jews and Protestants, Catholic and Muslim. It was a small and simple alter with a couple of kneelers. And every one of us lit a candle and in turn knelt down and said a prayer of thanksgiving.

As we stood up and looked around, we noticed a "star of hope," a relic, and a couple of pictures.

Danny said, "Oh, I see you already have a relic of St. Jude."

"No," the nun told him. "Actually, it's a relic of St. Clement."

Oh boy, that was it. Danny knelt down right there on the spot and started quietly weeping.

"What's this? Tell us what's the matter?"

"Somebody get me some water," he said.

"What's wrong?"

He stood up, grabbed a tissue to dab his eyes, and then told us about how he used to pray in Chicago to the statue of St. Jude in what he thought was St. Jude's Church. And as it turned out one day some little old lady informed him that indeed it was a statue of St. Jude that he was praying to, but the church he was in was St. Clement's.

"St. Clement is in our particular order," the nuns said. "And St. Clement is one of our favorite saints that we pray to. We thought you wouldn't mind if we put the relic of St. Clement here rather than the relic of St. Jude."

He took a sip from the glass he was handed and shook his head, "I can hardly believe the miracles that have been happening, and this is just another. Now, I know this hospital is just meant to be."

Book 2: Chapter 24: At the Banquet

Prior to dinner, Mike Tamer was acting as host and introducing people to each other.

One of the people he introduced me to was Abe Lastfogel, owner of the William Morris Talent Agency in Los Angeles.

In case you forgot, it was Abe Lastfogel that propelled Danny Thomas to stardom with a contract they signed back in 1943.

So, that was kind of a big deal for me to meet Mr. Lastfogel, me being a performer and all.

There were probably a half-a-dozen of us standing around chatting, when someone announced that it was almost dinner time and time to find a seat.

I was getting ready to grab a chair when Mike Tamer walks over to me and says, "Jim, how about giving us a little prayer, sing the Ave Maria."

"I think it would be more appropriate," I suggested, "if I sang 'Bless This House.' It fits in more with the occasion."

"Oh, that's good. Do that one."

So, I stood up, no microphone or anything and said, "We are here for a reason tonight, and that reason is the opening of this great new institution. I think it would be very appropriate, if I were to sing, or that Mike Tamer has asked me to sing 'Bless This House.'"

And so I did.

When I finished singing, the seat I had originally planned on sitting in was now occupied. So, I went to another table and took an empty seat. As the Good Lord would have it, I was sitting next to Mr. Lastfogel.

"Young man," he said to me, "you really like to sing, don't you?"

"Yes sir, I do."

"Do you do any professional singing?"

"Well, I would say semi-professional. I make pretty good grocery money at it."

"Do you do any traveling?"

"Sure. I sing not only in Peoria, but I travel to cities all around central Illinois, and Chicago, and some other major cities in the Midwest too. I also do special occasions, weddings and funerals. And I have my own radio show and television show."

"Great. Do you have any engagements in Chicago," he asked. "Say, coming up in the next month or two?"

"In fact, I do. I'll be singing with my partner Betty Ann Clayton."

"Do you have any solos?"

"Yeah. Oh, yeah."

"Okay, young man, next time you're singing in Chicago, would you write me a note and tell me where you are going to be? I'd like to have someone listen to you. I'd like to see what you do, and how you do it; and who knows maybe we'll have something for you."

"Okay. I've got some dates coming up at the Edgewater Beach Hotel. I'll get you the dates."

Opening of St. Jude, Memphis

On February 4, 1962, St. Jude Children's Research Hospital was formally opened with a wonderful Grand Opening ceremony.

Ed Barry was the Master of Ceremonies; Mrs. Condon sang the National Anthem; and Monsignor Shea gave the Invocation.

Several people stood up and gave speeches, including the Mayor of Memphis; Mike Tamer; the Governor of Tennessee; and Danny Thomas.

To a crowd of nearly nine-thousand, Danny told the story of Billy Johnson.

Hearing the story again was just as moving as when it actually happened. And there wasn't a dry eye anywhere.

Danny, true to his word, showed the audience Billy Johnson's half dollar and quarter which were in the cornerstone for all to see; and for the ages to remember.

On top of that cornerstone stood a ten-foot tall statue covered with a black drape. And at the end of his talk, which concluded the dedication ceremony, Danny unveiled this magnificent white marble statue of St. Jude Thaddeus: and in turn keeping the promise he'd made to St. Jude so many years ago.

Danny gave the drape a tug, and then the curtain dropped. He looked up at the statue and then up to the sky and as if struck with epiphany, and he cried out, "My God, my God, now I know why I was born!"

Book 2: Chapter 26: Six Weeks Later

Well, six weeks later, there I was, singing at the famous Edgewater Beach Hotel in Chicago.

I was performing that night with my singing partner, Betty Ann Clayton; and we were accompanied by our piano player Adelaide White.

We started the set off with a duet, then she'd sing a song; then I'd sing a song; then we'd pair back up again. The whole night kind of went like that.

Betty Ann was a very talented young lady, and we had been singing together for years, mostly traveling around the Midwest, performing at Lady's clubs and things like that.

Anyway, we did our program and received an enthusiastic standing ovation. It was quite a night.

But it got better.

As we were putting our stuff away, some guy walks up and says, "Hi, I work for William Morris. Mr. Lastfogel sent me over here to listen to you sing."

"I'm flattered," I said. "I'm glad you told me now instead of before. I probably would've been so nervous, I wouldn't have been able to sing."

He said, "You sure love to sing, don't you."

"Oh, I love it. I love it."

"Boy, get ready we are traveling, we are moving."

Now that was the exact thing Horace Heidt had said

to me a year earlier, "Boy, get ready, we are traveling."

Last year, I had won the Horace Heidt contest down at the Shrine Mosque.

Now for those of you that don't know, Horace Heidt was one of the more popular big band leaders, back in the days of radio; and later, when TV came around, he had a talent show. He discovered comedian Art Carney, and jazz giant Al Hirt, to name a few.

So, anyway, I had won the Horace Heidt contest at the Shrine Mosque here in Peoria. And Heidt, himself, personally ask me to go on tour with him.

But I said, "Wait a minute, wait a minute. Let's talk. I'm a married man. I've got four kids."

"Four kids? Oh."

I told him straight out, "I don't want to leave my family."

And now, I've got a representative from William Morris, telling me to pack my bags.

"Wow, four kids," the agent said. "Oh, my goodness. It's a tough business, no doubt. But I'm here to say to you, if you want to go, I'm confident you can make it in this business. And if you're ready to go, I'm sure the William Morris Agency would love to have you. We could even design programs around you."

I had already turned down a once in a lifetime opportunity with Horace Heidt. I wasn't so sure I wanted to turn this offer down so quickly. Maybe God was trying to tell me something? Maybe I was supposed to walk through this door and fulfill my dream of being a professional singer?

And if anybody could make the dream come true, it was Abe Lastfogel that was for certain.

"Let me think about it," I told the agent.

"And pray about it," I told myself.

"When you're ready," he said, "we're ready."

So I came back home to Peoria.

I consulted with some of my closest friends including Monsignor John Whelan; Bill Adams, who was the head of WEEK-TV; Father Livingston, and a few others.

"Is this what I should be doing," I asked each and every one of them, "leave my family and go out on the road?"

"It's kind of risky," was the general warning from some.

"If you want to do it, that's great," others said.

And finally, one of them said, "maybe you should be asking God what he wants you to be doing."

Now, that was some good advice.

I believe that God has certain designs for all of our lives.

Did I want to be like Danny Thomas, singing all over the country, all over the world, yeah, you bet I did.

But I did what I believe I was called to do. I stayed in Peoria, helped Trudy raise the kids, worked hard at the family business, and ceaselessly raised money for the children of St. Jude.

Speaking of the family business, new technological breakthroughs had the dry cleaning business changing so fast it was hard to keep up with.

By 1960, about half the population owned their own homes. And almost everyone who owned a home, had invested in a washing machine, despite the high cost; because, let's face it, laundry has to be done all of the time, daily sometimes, and it was just more convenient.

But it wasn't just the household washing machine that had improved things. There were new machines out on the market that made dry cleaning easier and more efficient for the businessman too. So, in 1962, I invested in some brand new, modern, dry cleaning equipment.

And wouldn't you know it, the ink had barely dried on the loan, when a new invention hit the market, do-it-yourself dry cleaning machines. Practically over night, they were installed in laundromats all across America.

And in the blink of an eye, we lost about one-third of our dry cleaning business.

Hard times had fallen on Maloof Cleaners. And I was losing money and in debt.

When I had trouble paying my bills, I turned to my brother Mitchell for help, but he wasn't able to help me out.

So, I turned to some of the well-to-do Lebanese grocers in town. But no one was willing to help me out.

Every week that passed, more and more anxiety grew.

"What to do?" I thought, "What to do?"

Normally, when a Lebanese person is in need of help, you ask the Lebanese community for that help.

It's like an unwritten rule, you stick together, help each other out. You know, it's that kind of thing.

Well, in this case, because no one in the Lebanese community could help me out, I had two choices: lose the business, or go ask somebody outside the community for help.

I decided to reach out to a friend of the family, a Jewish guy by the name of Michael Bork.

On a hot and stinky day, I went to Bork's office down at the Peoria junk yards.

"Michael," I said to him, "I need some help. If I default on the loans I have for this new equipment, I'm going to lose the family business."

"It's that serious?" he said.

"Yeah," I said, "It's that serious. Can you lend me a few thousand dollars?"

He pulled open his desk drawer. He pulled out his checkbook. He started writing on the check.

"Hey," I said, not knowing what I might be getting myself into, "can we talk about terms first?"

He just kept writing.

"How much do you need?" he asked.

"I'll pay you back," I insisted, "with interest. I'll pay you back, with interest"

"Shut your mouth," he said. "You're always helping people: helping those kids at St. Jude and all that. It's about time somebody did something for you. So, how much do you need? $2,000-3,000 dollars?"

"More like $5,000 dollars," I said, kind of embarrassed.

"Okay, $5,000 dollars," he nodded as he wrote the words on the check.

I tried to protest, to talk about interest and a repayment schedule and all of that stuff.

He just waved me off with a flick of his wrist. He wasn't going to hear any of it.

He handed me the check, no questions asked, and just said, "You pay me when you get it."

Wow. Talk about salvation.

Thanks to Michael Bork, we got the business back on solid ground. And I was able to pay him back within a few years.

A lot of that was due to the fact that Peoria was experiencing an economic boom. Everybody was working, so that was good for our business.

It seemed like about one-quarter of Peoria County was now employed by the Caterpillar Tractor Company. Caterpillar had its first billion dollar year that year, I believe.

And the big breweries, Hiram Walker and Pabst were turning out incredible numbers as well.

My former Spalding classmate, Bob Lehnhausen became Mayor of Peoria in 1965, and a fellow by the name of Max J. Lipkin served as the interim city manager.

BOOK 3

The Memoirs of Jim Maloof

Book 3: Chapter 1: **The New Ramada Inn**

In 1966 another friend of ours, Roy Demanes, built a beautiful brand new Ramada Inn Hotel here in Peoria. It was located downtown, just below St. Francis Hospital.

Well, a few weeks before it was set to open Roy calls me up and says, "If you can find a way to get Danny Thomas to come here for the Grand Opening, I will host a dinner for as many people as you can fit in our ballroom."

"How many?" I asked him; and, of course, "How much?"

"Jim," he says, "that's nearly three hundred people. It's free of charge: all the food, the banquet facilities; and we'll even furnish rooms, again, free of charge. I'll pay every penny of it; it won't cost you a cent."

"Well, that sounds like a deal I can't refuse, Roy, but first let me call Danny. I'll get back to you."

And the next day, I called Danny, and he agreed to come to Peoria.

Now, I just want to clarify for you, that by this time Danny Thomas was doing well; he was wealthy, famous, and had friends in high places. He'd started producing television shows back in the late 1950's, starting with *The Danny Thomas Show*. And then he had his hand in *The Andy Griffith Show*, followed by blockbuster hits like *Gomer Pyle*, and *The Dick Van Dyke Show*.

But despite all of his personal success, it was still difficult for him to continue to sell his project.

There were still so many naysayers out there, especially in the medical community. There were doctors and nurses and research specialist that just would not buy into Danny's dream. A lot of them thought it was some kind of hokes, you know, a celebrity running a free hospital. "Sure," they said with their skepticism, "good luck with that."

And I knew, from first hand experience their skepticism. I remember when Trudy made me go to Chicago, when I thought all Danny Thomas wanted was my money – which I didn't have.

But now, I got it.

The light had gone off in my head, like when Paul was struck on the road to Demascus.

Ninety-six out of every one-hundred kids diagnosed with leukemia were dying.

And we knew cancer wasn't going to cure itself. It takes people and money to cure diseases.

And so Danny came to share the message again.

Book 3: Chapter 2: An Incredible Party

The night Roy Demanes threw the party was incredible. He had the ballroom especially decorated for the occasion and served the finest food you could want.

The head table consisted of Tom Liston of Bergner's, the three hospital chairmen, representing Proctor, St. Francis, and Methodist, Danny Thomas and about ten others distinguished guests.

And even though I was the chairman of the event, that night I did something a little different, I turned the job of emcee over to my friend Michael Bork, who was also sitting at the head table.

So, anyway, he agreed to be the front man. And what a great decision that turned out to be. Michael Bork was absolutely hilarious that night. He wowed them, and killed them at the same time. Even Danny was buckled over with laughter.

You know, it was stuff like, "A rabbi, a priest and a monk walk into a bar. The bartender takes one look at them and says, 'What is this? A joke?'"

Or he'd throw out an old Jewish saying, like, "Always accept misfortune as a blessing and never wish for perfect health or a problem-free life. Why? Because what else would you have to talk about?"

It was good clean stuff.

And I must say, the chemistry in the room that night, it just had the making of something special.

Book 3: Chapter 3: The Importance of Hart

There were nearly 300 guests at the Ramada Inn that night. They were all decked out in their tuxedos and their finest gowns.

And most of them were from the local medical community: doctors, and nurses, and administrators, and so forth.

I would say that 85% of the people in the ballroom that night were medical people.

And that included Dr. Robert Hart, a pediatrician here in Peoria.

Dr. Hart was one of the very first pediatricians to suggest to his patients that they go to the research hospital in Memphis.

And it took courage to do that.

Why?

Because when St. Jude opened, it was a research hospital, trying to cure a disease that killed almost every child in its path.

So with the permission of the parents, new and experimental drugs were tried on the patients.

Normally, drug research was limited to testing on animals, but because the mortality rate was so incredibly high, parents and patient were willing to travel to try new and unconventional treatments in hope of easing the physical and emotional pain that accompanies the disease.

Some in the medical profession didn't want to be a part of a research hospital, where, so they thought, people were experimented on like guinea pigs.

But not Dr. Hart.

While others viewed the situation with negativity, Dr. Hart embraced it with optimism.

Where others saw only danger, Dr. Hart saw opportunity.

While others were fearful, Dr. Hart was hopeful.

While others did nothing, Dr. Hart persevered.

He had four patients that made the journey down to Memphis, all were cancer-stricken and all were surviving.

That night at the Ramada Inn, when Danny gave his speech, he talked about the courage of Dr. Hart, the courage of the families that made the 450 mile journey in hope of a cure; and the courage of the children.

Oh, he had them all teary-eyed, including me.

Living Proof

One courageous youth that made that trek from Peoria to Memphis was Clay Johnson.

When Clay was diagnosed with childhood cancer, he was only given about two weeks to live.

Immediately, his parents rushed him down to St. Jude Children's Research Hospital in Memphis. There, by the grace of God, Dr. Pinkel and his staff were able to save Clay's life.

Clay Johnson went on to become the valedictorian of his class at Woodruff.

And after high school, he went to the University of Illinois, where he was an honors student; and after that, he went to Syracuse, where he studied law and graduated summa cum laude.

Twice he served as a judicial clerk, once in New York, and then in Kansas City for the United States Court of Appeals.

He practiced law in Missouri, Kansas, and New York.

After about ten years in the legal profession, Clay decided to attended Covenant Theological Seminary.

He's married now, has four children, and wants to show his thanks to the Lord by working as a minister and serving others.

The Embryo of an Idea

When Danny got on a roll, nobody could talk the talk like he could.

And that night at the Ramada Inn, oh, the ballroom was on fire. The people were enthusiastic about what he was saying; about Dr. Hart and the research that would keep children alive and healthy; and all that stuff.

He mentioned the great job Peoria was doing, financially. We had raised almost a quarter of a million dollars over the last three years for St. Jude.

And then he said, "With the money you are raising here in Peoria, with the cooperation you're getting from the medical community, wouldn't it be great if someday we had an affiliate?

"After all, St. Jude just can't be for Memphis people only, it has got to be for the children of the country, of the world."

Later that night, there were about four of us, sitting around talking over a vodka and tonic.

And Danny leaned over toward me and said, "Hey, I've never seen this kind of support from the medical community anywhere in the United States."

"Yeah," I said, "Peoria really believes in its children."

"Taking into consideration what you have done

here," he said, "I think Peoria would be a great candidate for the first affiliate in the country."

"Danny," I said, "you get Dr. Pinkel's approval and help us build it. We'll raise the money."

The Next Step

So after Danny left Peoria, he arranged for a meeting in Washington, D.C., with the National Institute of Health – the NIH.

I mean, you can't just say, "I'm going to open a clinic." You have to get approval.

The plans were made, and so, Danny, Dr. Pinkel, myself, and a few others flew out to have a meeting with some of NIH people.

We also met with Dr. Frank Rauscher, Jr., one of the top scientists at the National Cancer Institute – the NCI.

St. Jude was tough gains, taking baby steps, but still there was another portion of the medical community, while not wanting to be involved, that wanted to know the results of the treatments and procedures Dr. Pinkel was implementing.

The findings of the doctors and research scientists at St. Jude were always being written up in the medical journals. So the NIH and the NCI, they knew exactly what we were trying to accomplish at St. Jude: thorough research, one treatment at a time, one child at a time, with love, compassion, and honesty.

And by the end of our meeting, we had the full support of Dr. Rauscher.

He said, "I have no doubt this is a good thing. Dr. Pinkel, if you believe you can assist and monitor the affiliate, I'd go for it if I were you."

Book 3: Chapter 7: Trying to Find a Home

After returning from Washington, D.C., I called a meeting with St. Francis, Methodist, and Proctor – the three hospitals here in Peoria.

I sat down with the three administrators and told them what had transpired between Rauscher, Pinkel, and myself.

My original thought, I explained, was for the three hospitals to come together and build a freestanding institution somewhere here in Peoria.

So, as we wrapped up the meeting, I said, "Okay, that's the plan. It's only an idea, it's a beginning, and I want to put the ball in your court."

The following day, Don Vaughn, the head of Methodist, called me and said, "Hey, Jim, we're interested. Even if the other two hospitals don't want to do it, we'd like to talk further."

I went back to St. Francis and Proctor, but couldn't get any more interest out of either of them.

So I put the ball in Methodist's hands and put them in touch with Memphis.

The President of the Trustees for Methodist Hospital, at that time, was a guy by the name of Clarence Yordy.

It was Clarence who really opened up the dialogue. He would call Memphis asking a lot of questions.

He wanted to know exactly what it would take to start an affiliate; he wanted to know how it would work, and who would raise the money. Was it to be a hospital outside of a hospital? It was all these kinds of questions Clarence Yordy was asking.

Of course, as Dr. Rauscher originally pointed out, Memphis would have to be in full control of an affiliate, if we wanted to pass the NIH. That much we knew.

Yordy and the Methodist people made several trips to Memphis to find out even more, hands on. And Memphis sent people here to talk to Methodist.

This went on for a year and five months, until finally, Clarence said, "Jim, it looks like we're going to get it done."

And I said, "Lordy, Lordy. Thank God for Clarence Yordy."

Word was getting out on the street that Peoria was maybe going to get an affiliate.

And now, I get a call from Ed McGrath, the head of St. Francis. He was irate, I mean, he was really upset.

"What's this business of your doing? You're going to give Methodist the affiliate? I thought you were talking to all of us?"

I said, "Ed. That was a year and a half ago. You didn't move; they did. They've had people in Memphis; Memphis people have come up and visited Methodist. They've got the whole package together. If you really want to push this, then my advice for you, now, is to talk to Memphis."

"I'm talking to you!"

"Ed, my hands are tied. They've got something going on and if it's going to change, it'll have to be through Memphis. It's not my call."

He said, "I want you to know, one: you know that affiliate ought to be in a Catholic institution."

Whoops, strike one.

"No," I said, "The St. Jude Affiliate, just like in Memphis, has no bars on any youngster from any religion: it's open to anyone."

"Well, number two: if we don't get that affiliate, we are going to quit doing business with your company."

Whoops, strike two.

"Ed," I said, "since when do we mix professional business with community business?"

"Well, that's the way it's going to be," he said.

"Okay," I told him, "it's your call, Ed McGrath. The only thing I can tell you, Ed, is a name and phone number to call down in Memphis."

Book 3: Chapter 10: **An Emergency Meeting**

Immediately, I got on the phone and called Clarence.

I said, "Clarence, how close are we to an agreement with Memphis?"

"Oh, we've got it," he said. "The only thing we are waiting on now is a meeting of Peoria people and Memphis people – and we've got the deal."

And I said, "Don't let me rattle your cage, but look, I just finished a phone call with Ed McGrath. And if Methodist wants an affiliate, after working all this time, you better get me an 'okay' by tomorrow."

"Tomorrow?"

"Yep. Otherwise, you are at risk. Not me: you are at risk."

So, Clarence called an emergency meeting of the executive committee of the Methodist Hospital Trustees.

It was around dinner time, the same day, about 5 o'clock, when he called and said, "It's a done deal. We've talked to Memphis, and we've got this whole thing wrapped up. You've got yourself an affiliate."

"No," I said, "the community has an affiliate. The community has an affiliate."

Methodist and Memphis began working on the

paperwork, procedures, and everything. There was finally going to be a St. Jude Children's Research Hospital affiliate in Peoria, Illinois.

And being the first one of its kind, we all knew there was a lot more work ahead; it wouldn't happen over night, but this was a great start.

Book 3: Chapter 11: Dry Cleaning is Drying Up

By the end of 1967, I had eleven dry cleaning offices in and around the Peoria area. I had a total of sixty employees. And I made about $27,000 dollars that year.

Now, that wasn't bad money for the '60's, but it was hard, tiring, physical labor.

And while the dry cleaning business wasn't as grueling as it had been when my dad started out, or when I was a young man, we still were sweating like dogs and working our butts off.

And then I'd hear about these guys who were going over to Caterpillar and making the same as me, pushing some broom around, sweeping floors all day.

I was pushing 47-years old. And I thought to myself, I don't want to continue to work this hard for the rest of my life, not when people are doing a lot less for the same money or more.

So, I began thinking, maybe I should get out of the dry cleaning business and do something else?

I knew I couldn't go over to Caterpillar and sweep floors. From my parents I had inherited that Lebanese entrepreneurial spirit; I couldn't work for anybody else. It just wasn't in my blood.

My brother Mitchell, who had also inherited that entrepreneurial spirit, had gotten out of the used car business many years ago and had started selling commercial real estate. He was a one-man operation, and he was doing pretty good at it.

"Maybe I should give that a try?" I thought.

It would be a major life change, because the cleaning business was all I knew how to do.

It might be difficult for me to learn something new, and I wasn't exactly a young man anymore. Mitchell told me that to sell real estate, I'd have to pass tests and stuff like that. And I didn't have anything but a high school education. I hadn't studied for a test in thirty years.

And then there was the question, did I want to give up the business which my dad had started? The business which bore the family name?

These were tough questions for me: questions which Trudy and I spent many a night talking over and over, again and again.

Book 3: Chapter 12: **Major Changes**

While I was feeling some inner turbulence in my own life, there was a lot more in the outside world.

In the spring of '68, Martin Luther King, Jr., was shot. And then in the summer Bobby Kennedy was killed. And things continued to get worse as the anti-war protesters were clashing with the police into the fall. Things seemed to be getting out of hand.

Apparently, all the craziness was enough to push people to drink, because here at home Pabst Brewery rolled out a record 5 million barrels of beer that year.

As for me, I was more involved with St. Jude than ever before. I was elected Second Vice President of ALSAC, which was a pretty big honor for a little guy like me. It was a two year deal.

My new role meant that I'd be doing even more traveling in my efforts to raise money for St. Jude. In other words, it wasn't limited to just the Midwest, as it had been before.

Trudy and I finally came to a decision about the business. Together, we decided it was time to take the plunge. I would sell Maloof Cleaners and try my hand at real estate.

I sold the business contract-for-deed, which

basically meant that I was the bank. I was the one loaning the buyers the money to purchase the business.

The guys I sold it to paid me $5,000 dollars upfront, and then agreed to make payments until it was paid off. You know, like any other kind of loan, we set up a fixed amount and dates the payments were due on, and that kind of thing.

I stayed at home and studied for my real estate salesman's license. And a few months later, I went down to Springfield to take the test.

Lo and behold, I could hardly believe it, I passed with flying colors.

Then in the fall, I started studying for my broker's license.

With my salesman's license, I was qualified to sell real estate, but if I was able to get my broker's license, then I'd be able to go into business for myself.

By November, my brother Mitchell had agreed to give me a little closet space in his office, so I could start selling real estate.

And that's what I did.

Book 3: Chapter 13: Annual Christmas Sing

The holidays have always been a special time for the Maloof family: especially around Christmas time. And in 1968, I was asked to be the song leader for the Annual Christmas Sing. What an honor.

Next to going to church on Sunday with your family, I think singing Christmas carols together as a community is the best way to celebrate the holiday.

The Christmas sing was started by Howard Kellogg back in 1948. And every year, I'd drag the whole family down to the courthouse, so we could sing along.

The first year I was asked to be the song leader, there were about 200 people that showed up.

We had given everyone a candle to hold, and it was already dark when we lit them. And as we were singing "Silent Night," ah, here comes the snow.

And I tell you, there was just something so spiritual about that. It was as if God was letting us know that he was listening.

By the way, the Annual Christmas sing continues on to this day. And in all of these years, it has only had two song leaders: Howard Kellogg and yours truly.

Starting on my Own

That winter, I was having lunch with a friend of mine, Ralph Kent.

Ralph worked at Commercial Bank, and we had done business together before. But on this occasion, we were just shooting the breeze about family, friends, the holiday, and whatnot.

Anyway, I was telling him that I had got my real estate salesman's license, when he interrupted me and said, "Jim, Why don't you go into business for yourself?"

"Well," I started to explain, "I don't have my broker's license yet. And even then it's going to take some time, because I don't have any money saved up."

He said, "I'll lend you the money. When you're ready, I'll lend you the money."

Come February, I went to Springfield once again. And once again, I passed the test.

Now, I had my broker's license. Hallelujah!

So, I called Ralph Kent back up, and he set me up with a loan for $3,000 to start my own realty company.

And while my brother Mitchell was a very good mentor, I couldn't wait to get out on my own.

I packed up the few things I had on the desk, and thanked him for all the help and encouragement he'd given me over the past year.

My new office would be a little rented 8' x 10' out

on North University. I hired a very part-time secretary and put my shingle out for business.

The birth of Jim Maloof Realty, in February 1969, was not particularly auspicious. Like everything else in life, there was no harbinger or town crier in the square ringing a bell to make the announcement to the world.

Our lives are not made by flamboyant maneuvers and pronouncements, rather we make our lives by the simple, small, mundane decisions of every day living.

We pray to God, and we work hard.

The first property I ever sold, by the way, was on Kellogg Terrace, and I've sold that property four times since.

Book 3: Chapter 15: My Brother Mitchell

My brother Mitchell was one of the most unique men I have ever known in my entire life. You just had to know him to love him.

He had one of the most unusual offices. Every lawyer and judge in Peoria visited his office at least once a week. He probably had 15-20 different kinds of candy sitting in dishes on the counter there. And these guys would walk in, say "Hi", take same candy and leave.

He hired the secretaries that were connected. He knew how to get things done. Stories still surface wherever I go. He made an indelible impression everywhere he went.

He was great with the kids, my kids loved him. He always had pistachio nuts and the candies in his office. He was a very generous and giving uncle.

One time he had his office right on top of a toy store, the kids loved that. It was like Disneyland every time we went over to visit.

Before he got into real estate, he was a used car salesman down on Adams. He was known as "Madman Maloof." And he ran ads in the newspaper under that name. No question about it, he was crafty.

My mother was now living with my brother Mitchell, his wife Delores, and their kids.

Mom was getting older, and we thought it was best if she no longer lived by herself. The neighborhood we grew up in was always a little rough, which was okay when we had safety in numbers, but it wasn't the place for an aging single woman, no matter how strong she was.

She'd lost an eye about ten years ago. This is a true story.

When my dad had been admitted to St. Francis Hospital, back in '59, she, of course, went to visit him every day.

It was summertime, and she was standing on Glen Oak Avenue, just outside of St. Francis, waiting to catch the bus, when a bug flew in her eye.

Well, she rubbed it and rubbed it and rubbed it.

The next day, when she went to see dad, she stopped by the nurse's station and told them what had happened. They looked at it and flushed it out and all of that stuff, and told her she'd be alright.

But, she wouldn't stop rubbing it.

And this went on for weeks, literally. Nobody could get her to stop rubbing her eye – and eventually, she went blind in that eye.

So with that, and her health somewhat on the

decline she agreed to move in with Mitchell and his family, over there on University.

They took good care of her and were a real blessing.

But around the beginning of March she had taken ill, and had to be omitted to Saint Francis Hospital.

Then, on April 1st, 1969, my mother, Sarah Zyne Maloof, passed away.

The last words she spoke to me, as she lay dying, were *go help the children & God help you.*

Mrs. Sarah Maloof

Obituary from the Peoria Journal Star, Wednesday, April 2, 1969, A.M. Edition –

Mrs. Sarah Maloof, 78, a resident of 3602 N. University St. for the last 18 months and of Peoria for 62 years died at 12:45 p.m. yesterday at St. Francis Hospital where she had been a patient for four weeks.

Born in Fizul, Lebanon, August 15, 1890, she was the daughter of Mr. and Mrs. Abraham Zyne, and was married to Nimer Maloof in New York City in November 1907. He died in Peoria June 3, 1959. She was a member of St. Philomena's Catholic Church, the Catholics Women's League and the American Lebanese Syrian Society.

Surviving are fours sons, Mitchell J. Maloof, with whom she had been making her home, and James A. Maloof, both of Peoria. Abraham J. Maloof of Indianapolis, Ind., and Fred M. Maloof of Washington, D.C.: 14 grandchildren and five great grandchildren.

Services will be at 10 a.m. tomorrow at Wilton Mortuary. The Rev. Joseph I. Gerber and the Rev. Robert C. Livingston will officiate and burial will be in St. Joseph's Cemetery.

Friends may call the mortuary from 4 to 9 p.m. today. The Catholics Women's League Rosary will be recited there at 3:30 p.m. and the parish Rosary at 8 p.m.

Memorial contributions may be sent to the St. Jude Children's Research Hospital.

Even though the Memphis people and the Peoria people agreed on an affiliate, it took three years to get all the formalities out of the way.

The last step was to get final approval from the national board of directors in Memphis. They had to vote on it.

It seemed like there was always one more hoop to jump through.

The meeting was held in the summer of 1969 in Houston, Texas.

There were whispers, even before the meeting began, that several of the national board members were not in favor of an affiliate.

"We're not a franchise."

"We're not some fast food joint."

And two of the board members in particular were against it. One was a guy, I remember very well, he was from Chicago.

And when the floor was opened up for discussion, this guy from Chicago stood up and just railed and railed against the opening of an affiliate; not just in Peoria, but anywhere.

The more he talked, you could just see people nodding in agreement with him. He had just about everybody convinced.

"This is not the thing to do," I remember him saying as he pounded his fist on the table.

"Oh, Lord have mercy," I said, glancing up.

And it was just about this time, out of the corner of my eye, I saw Danny Thomas sneaking in the back door. I'm sure that had it gone to a vote, right there and then, it would have been turned down.

And so, I said, "Mr. Chairman, order of business, may I ask for a two minute recess?"

"Yes," he said, "you may have a five minute recess."

The Chairman was Ed Barry. And I think he knew why I wanted a recess. And he granted it, because he too wanted the affiliate.

I ran back to Danny.

Naturally, he'd missed all proceedings, and he was all excited about the affiliate. He thought it was just the greatest thing in the world.

"Yes," he said, "are they ready to pass the vote?"

"No," I said. "That guy from Chicago is trying to kill it. He's railing against it so bad that I'm sure if we took a vote right now, it's dead in the water."

Well, Danny uttered some words of profanity that said something like, "Up front. Let's go. Let's call this meeting back to order." Oh boy, was he cussing his head off as we went back to the meeting table.

I said, "Mr. Chairman, we are ready to resume the meeting."

And Ed Barry called the meeting back to order.

"If you please, Mr. Chairman," I said, "Mr. Thomas

would like to speak on the subject of an affiliate in Peoria."

Danny got up and spoke as if the good Lord had found phrases and words for him.

He pointed his finger at some of those people, in effect, calling them out.

He spoke for about fifteen minutes. He talked about why St. Jude should be helping not only the children in Memphis, but the children of the world. And that now was the time to open those doors.

Wow, he was just tremendous.

And when he finished, there wasn't a word said.

"Anyone want to speak?" the chairman asked. "Anyone else want to talk on the subject?"

Again, not a single person said a word.

Then I spoke up, "Mr. Chairman, may I call for a roll call vote?"

The vote was unanimous.

And with that vote, the first St. Jude affiliate was on its ways to becoming a reality.

In the thirty-five years that I was with Danny, it was the most magical, glorifying, God-inspired speech I ever heard in my entire life.

I was in Bloomington, Illinois, speaking at an American Legion function about St. Jude. I was telling them about the Teen March, and the fact that we had been approved for an affiliate that was going to be located in Peoria.

This was on a Sunday evening in October of 1969.

Shortly after I had arrived home, and got ready to crawl into bed, then the phone rang.

It was about midnight and I about jumped out of my bedroom slippers trying to grab the phone before it woke the whole darn house up.

"Mr. Maloof?"

"Yes?" I said, a little groggy from the sleep I was thinking about falling into.

"You don't know me, but I just heard you speak at the American Legion in Bloomington earlier tonight, and I want to invite you to speak in Chicago, later this month, to a ladies' group called ESA."

I said, "Woman, why would you be calling me at midnight?"

"Well," she said, "I'm just so excited, Mr. Maloof. I just found out that I could invite you to speak at our convention."

"Uh-huh?" I said.

"So, I wanted to call now. Honestly, Mr. Maloof, you'll never have this opportunity again."

And I said, "Who are you? And who are you speaking for?"

Honestly, I was as confused as could be. I've heard it said, "Why wait until tomorrow, what you can do today," but this was ridiculous.

"I'm so sorry," she said. "Didn't I introduce myself? My name is Marilyn Knuth. And I'm speaking for the ESA: Epsilon Sigma Alpha"

While I said something polite in return, my brain said, "Who the heck is ESA?"

"Oh, you haven't heard?"

"No."

"Mr. Maloof," she continued with great enthusiasm, "ESA is a civic-minded non-collegiate sorority founded in 1929. There are over 30,000 members throughout the United States."

Okay, now she was gaining my attention.

"And there are chapters in just about every state in the Union. We raise money for philanthropic causes. Our chapter, here in the state of Illinois, has been raising money for the Heart Association for years. I just think our members ought to hear the story of St. Jude. Maybe they'll agree to adopt St. Jude as our number one agency?"

Wow. Now she definitely had my attention.

"So, you think you might like to raise some money for St. Jude?" I said.

"Well, our members will have to vote on it, Mr. Maloof. This is just an opportunity for St. Jude, but I think it's a good one."

"And how many people will be there at this meeting?" I asked her.

"Since this is our state convention, we would expect a crowd of about 800 women. Again, it's in Chicago, the third Saturday in October."

"Ah, my birthday," I thought.

The last time I was invited to Chicago around my birthday, it turned out pretty well. So, I said, "Okay, put me down. I'll be there."

"Great," she said. "Don't be late. The lady president will only give you a certain amount of minutes to speak. So you have to be there right on time."

As it turned out, the third Saturday in October of 1969, was my 50th birthday. Wow, now there really was something to look forward to.

Trudy and I left for the ESA convention in Chicago around 5:30 in the morning. I figured that would give us plenty of time.

We got about as far as Bloomington, when it started raining. We went a little further and it got worse and worse.

Pretty soon it was raining so bad that we had to pull off to the side of the road because the windshield wipers wouldn't move the water away fast enough for us to see.

We stopped for about 15 minutes, until it finally slowed down enough to continue.

Next, we get about as far as Pontiac, when the heavy rains started again. And the same thing, we pull off to the side and waited for it to lighten up.

We were sitting there a long time, again. Finally, I said to Trudy, "Let's go home?"

"No," she said.

"Now come on this isn't worth it," I insisted. "I'm going to be late as it is, and there is no guarantee that I'll even get to speak if we're late."

"No," she said, "you promised you'd be there."

"Okay," I said.

When the rain slowed, off we went.

Finally, we get up as far as Joliet, and the downpour hits us again, for the third time now.

"All right!" I said, shaking my finger up at the sky. "That is it."

I pulled off the road again, and told Trudy, "We are going back home."

She reached over and pulled the keys out of the ignition.

"Alright, big mouth," she said, "you made a promise, and you're going to keep it. You made a promise that you were going to be there, and by heavens, we are going to go. I don't care if it rains all day. You are going to be there!"

When the rain slowed down, she gave me back the keys. I quietly put them in the ignition and we headed up to Chicago.

Through the rain and the fog we finally arrive in Chicago sometime after 10 o'clock.

"Trudy, could you go park the car?" I said. "I'll run inside."

Yes, Trudy could drive now, what a blessing, it made life much easier: with grandkids needing to be shuttled here, and there, and whatnot.

Anyway, while she parked the car, I ran into the hotel to let them know that we were here.

I went into the lobby, where I stopped to ask for directions. A group of ladies overheard me, and became very excited.

"Jim Maloof?" one of the ladies asked.

It turned out to be Marilyn Knuth and a couple of other gals. And as the good Lord would have it, I hadn't missed my turn. I told her that Trudy would be right in, and then we'd be ready to go.

"No. No," she said. "You come with me. One of the other girls will show her the way. Come on, this way. Hurry up. You're going to be on at 10:30 a.m."

It was now about 10:25 a.m.

"And if you miss it," she warned me, "there won't be another opportunity."

As we stepped into the elevator, she told me everything that happened up to that point.

"Someone from the Heart Association has already spoken; there was a small break; and now another gentleman from another nonprofit is on stage, right now."

As the elevator went up, she gave me the run down of the rules.

"Are you ready?"

"Yes, Ma'am, I'm ready," I told her.

As we walked into the room, the president spotted us and said, "I believe our next guest speaker is now ready. Mr. Maloof, would you like to come up and speak?"

"Yes, Ma'am," I said to her, "I'm ready."

And as I was walking toward the podium, she continued to address me. "Now, Mr. Maloof, I want to caution you. We are on a very tight schedule. There is a woman in the front row with a stopwatch. And you have exactly six minutes to give your message. Six minutes, okay?"

Six minutes? I don't remember anybody saying anything about six minutes.

"Oh, my heavens," I thought, "how am I going to do this?"

I took my place behind the podium.

I looked out over a crowd of some 600-plus women.

I introduced myself and said, "I can't even blow my nose in six minutes." And there was a little bit of a chuckle.

"Ladies of ESA, I want to thank you for having me. As you know, I have six minutes to tell you about this wonderful cause, St. Jude. But look, on the way up here, I found out some very interesting stories about your Madame President, would you like to hear them? There might be a little dirt in some of them?"

"Oh, yeah," they said.

So first, I gave them a few funny one-liners, and they laughed and clapped.

Then, I peeled off about six or seven more one-liners, mixed in with a few short stories about their Madame President. They were applauding and having a good laugh. And the Madame President, she was laughing too.

And then the lady with the stop watch went to cut me off. Heck, I hadn't even mentioned St. Jude yet.

"Madame President," I begged, "what am I to do?"

The ladies were shouting, "Let him talk."

And the Madame President said, "We'll give you an extra five minutes. You had six minutes, now I'll give you an extra five minutes."

I kept tossing out zingers, and the audience was just going nuts.

And then I'd stop and say, "This is your meeting. This is your time, do you want me to keep going?"

And this time the crowd overruled the president, but she was enjoying it too much to refuse.

"Mr. Maloof, go ahead now, we're going to let you speak for just a few moments more."

So, I told my favorite stories about Danny and his promise to St. Jude; about Billy Johnson; about the research; and the news of the affiliate.

Heck, it was about twenty-five minutes later when

Birth of an Affiliate

Press conference in December of 1971 announcing the start of
St. Jude services at Methodist Hospital in Peoria, Illinois.

seated right to left: **Jim Maloof**; **Donald K. Larson**, Associate Administrator;
and **Clarence Yordy**.

below: **Dr. Moris A. Adland**, **Danny Thomas**, **Clarence Yordy**, and **Jim Maloof**
celebrate the opening of the St. Jude Midwest Afflilate clinic.

The Telethon

above: **Jim Maloof** and **Vic Burnett** host the first telethon.

Tom Liston of P.A. Bergner & Co.; **Jim Maloof**, and **Bill Adams** of WEEK-TV.

THE TELETHON COULD NOT HAPPEN WITHOUT THE HELP OF THE MANY, MANY VOLUNTEERS.

above: In this photograph you can see **Dr. John Taraska** *(top left, leaning forward)*; shop **Edward O'Rourke** *(front row, about to hang up the phone)*; **Dave Ryan** of Dave and Erie's Lums *(with mustache)*; and **Dr. Robert Hart** *(far right, taking a pledge)*.

below: The WEEK-TV news team visits the telethon.

(l to r): **Jim Maloof, Clark Smith, Rollie Keith,** om **McIntyre,** and **Norm Ulrich** with **Vic Burnett**.

Ann Jillian

Golden Globe Winning Actress →

Roger Monroe

← ## Phil Donahue

Emmy-Winning Media Personality

below: **Jim Maloof** and **Bill Adams**

The Annual Christmas Sing

Silver bells, silver bells
It's Christmas time in the city
Ring-a-ling, hear them ring
Soon it will be Christmas day

...f street lights,
...p lights
...bright... ...green.

Photo credit: Ron Johnson used by permission of the Peoria Journal Star

Life Long Friends & Fishing Buddies

Nick Bourazak   Jim Barrack

Jim Maloof

Louis Ayoub

left: At the
Mayor's cook-off.
**Jim Maloof,
George Shadid,**
and
Pete Vonachan.

right:
**Pete Vonachan,
Father
Livingston,**
and
Chef Jim.

left: **Jim,**
at home,
preparing
Thanksgiving
dinner.

Friends of Friedrichshafen

Trudy and "**Der singen Burgomeister**" in Friedrichshafen, Germany - Peoria's Sister City - in 1989. They are enjoying the hospitality of The Mayor of Friedrichshafen and his wife.

Jim Maloof and Gene Farris

The Faces of
St. Jude

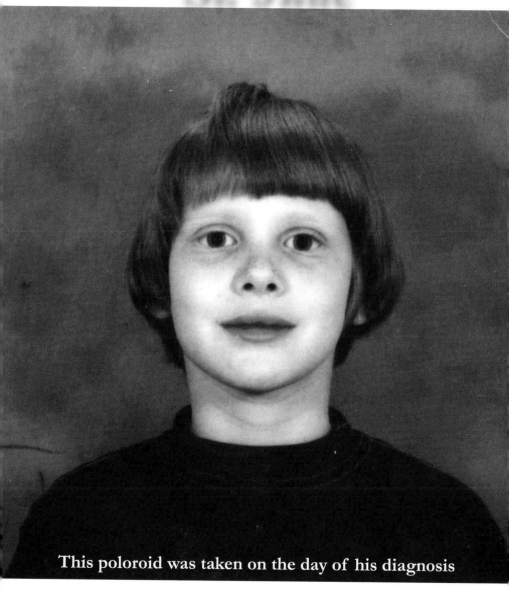

This poloroid was taken on the day of his diagnosis

Clay Johnson was only given two weeks to live...

One year later

Jim and **Clay** celebrate on Clay's wedding.

Today: Clay Johnson and his family

Amy McClellan-Jones

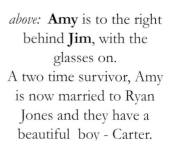

above: **Amy** is to the right behind **Jim**, with the glasses on.
A two time survivor, Amy is now married to Ryan Jones and they have a beautiful boy - Carter.

Dusty Paulter

"If **Dusty** had not lost his battle with leukemia, I honestly believe he would have gone on to become the next St. Jude Spokesman. He just had that kind of sparkle and passion in his personality." *(r)* **Joy Paulter** kisses **Jim** at the 2010 Dedication.

above: **Bucky Jockisch**; U.S. Secretary of Transportation **Raymond H. LaHood**; **Jim Maloof**; and **Bob Jockisch**.

Richard Unes

Senator George Shadi⟨

The 2011 President of ALSAC

above: **Jim** with a few of his fellow **South-West Kiwanis** members.

below: **Mayor Maloof** with **Sam Black, Dick Zych,** and **Bill Rinehart** at Caterpillar Family Day - June 8, 1996.

DAVID L. MCKEE
ALSAC CEO

MIKE MCCOY

Marshall and Nancy
Lipkin

JIM & TRUDY MALOOF
ST. JUDE MIDWEST
AFFILIATE CLINIC

DR. KAY SAVING

I concluded.

And as I wrapped it up, right there on the spot, I burst out into *Let there be Peace on Earth*. I took that song, and I blended it in with the song *I Believe*. And Oh, my heavenly days, there were tears all over the place.

When I was done, the Madame President thanked me and said, "If you will wait out in the lobby, we'll give you our decision shortly."

But before I could leave, they called for a vote right there and then.

And the place broke up and went crazy.

I didn't know what to do, and nobody said anything to me, so I slowly continued towards the doorway while I was watching all this commotion.

I had just walked out of the room, when here comes the lady from Bloomington, Marilyn Knuth, and a few other gals.

"We just adopted St. Jude as the philanthropic project for ESA Illinois," she said. "We can probably raise about $60,000 dollars for you over the next year."

Wow. That really made me happy. And she was so happy, she had tears all welled up in her eyes. And she kept thanking me and thanking me for coming to speak.

I, of course, had to thank Trudy and thank God because with out them, I wouldn't have even been here: I would have been at home getting ready for my 50th birthday party.

Proof again, that many times in life God will put you where you need to be, if it's your intent or not.

As Trudy and I were standing there talking to Marilyn Knuth and her little group, an attractive lady, probably in her mid-forties, came up to me and said, "Mr. Maloof?"

"Yes?"

"My name is Arlene Schloffer. I'm from St. Paul, Minnesota. And I will be the ESA International president in '71. I was really touched and moved by the work of St. Jude. Do you think it's possible that we could get Danny Thomas to St. Paul for our national convention, in June? June of '71, that is."

Well, that was more than a year and a half from now. So, I said, "Certainly, we'll try. God willing, we'll see what we can do."

"If you can get Danny Thomas to come to our national convention, I assure you, we will give you every consideration on becoming a national project."

"Oh, my gracious," I said, "You aren't kidding."

"No."

"Like I said, if you can get him here, we'll do everything we can to make St. Jude our ESA International project."

I had also received speaking invitations from other ESA state conventions.

So over the next year and a half, I hit the road with Marilyn Knuth and a couple of other ladies.

We told the St. Jude story in Madison, Wisconsin; Davenport, Iowa; Springfield, Missouri; Indianapolis, Indiana; Columbus, Ohio; and at a couple of other conventions.

I'd always conclude my talk with "Let There be Peace on Earth." And in every case, they'd adopt St. Jude as their state philanthropy.

And every time we'd get one locked up, I'd call Danny and Mike Tamer and say, "Hey, one more guys. One more. And don't forget June '71, Danny, don't forget."

After the first one or two, he'd just say, "Okay, I'll be there."

But after I'd locked up the entire Midwest, he said, "Don't worry. I'm going to be there. If it's that good, I'm going to be there for sure!"

Things were going well for me, and my part in helping St. Jude; especially with ESA.

In 1970 I was elected First Vice President of the Board of Directors for ALSAC. It was another two year term, and with increased responsibilities. I was on the go again, and I was raising a lot of money for the children of St. Jude and loving every minute of it.

And so it Burned Down

It took about a year from the time I sold the dry cleaning business until the new owners burned it to the ground.

Out of the goodness of my heart, I had sold it to them contract-for-deed with a $5,000 dollar down payment.

I'm sure it was an accident, like they said, but, in the face of this disaster they simply gave me the property back and split.

So now, I'm left with a burned out building, and I'm out $40,000 dollars.

And to top it off, looters picked through the rubble and took anything that was left.

I was pretty upset about the whole thing. What a mess. And I was going to have to pay to get it cleaned up.

Let's be honest, there are times in life when we just don't understand what God is doing.

This wasn't the first time I'd asked that question, and it wouldn't be the last.

"Whenever I tried to become wise and learn what goes on in the world, I realized that you could stay awake night and day and never be able to understand what God is doing. However hard you try, you will never find out. The wise may claim to know, but they don't."

--*Ecclesiastes 8:16-17* (*The Good News Translation*)

For the ESA International Convention we had the banquet planned for a Friday night, with Danny's formal presentation scheduled shortly after dinner.

I took care of all the arrangements, bought his airline ticket, and had coordinated everything with his secretary, Betty. We were good to go.

Then comes Tuesday of that week, and I get a phone call from Danny.

He's talking in very whispered tones. "Hey, I can't make it. I can't make it to St. Paul this weekend."

I said, "Whoa. What's wrong? Why not?"

"I don't have a voice. I can't be in St. Paul on Friday."

"But Danny, they've been expecting you now for over a year."

"My doctor says I can't go out of town. I can't do anything. He says I shouldn't even be talking to you."

"Danny, you can't do this," I said in uncertain protest. "We've got 3,000 women coming from all over America to see you."

"Yeah, Jim, but I can't make it."

I said, "Why don't you go see your doctor again, and I'll call you tomorrow."

I called on Wednesday: turns out he's in worse

shape than on Tuesday.

Immediately, I got on his case, and we both exchanged some not-so-friendly words.

Finally, I said to him, "Danny, you just can't miss this opportunity. This is one of the biggest things that will ever happen to St. Jude."

I mean, the states I had locked up were going to bring in about a half a million dollars a year to St. Jude. And if we could lock up ESA International, we could more than double that, easy.

And it was killing me to think of all the money on the table we might be losing out on. But I didn't know what else to say to him, he knew the importance of it.

So, I let him go. "I'll call you tomorrow," I said.

"Listen, would you," he said in a low raspy yell, "I can't make it."

He put me back through to Betty, and she said, "Jim, I know we've got to have him there. And I'll do everything in my power to get him on that airplane."

Now comes Thursday.

"Betty. How is he doing?"

"Well, he's a little better, I think."

"What do you mean, 'I think?'"

"We're working on him, Jim. His wife, Rose Marie, and I are both working on him. Why don't you call me back a little bit later and I'll let you know how it's going."

Around 5 o'clock, I called her back.

"Guess what," she said.

"What?"

"I think he's warming up to the idea. Now he's starting to ask about what time the airplane leaves and things like that."

"Keep on him Betty. Keep on him."

I'm feeling like I'm in a real pickle. Here it is Thursday night, and I still don't know if he's going to show or not.

I go to bed that night praying, "Lord, let him come through."

3,000 Ladies All Dressed Up

And as the Good Lord would have it, Friday morning, I get a call from Betty.

"Guess What? Guess What? He's coming."

And as sure as heck, about 4 o'clock, he's landing at the St. Paul airport.

I'd gone over to the airport with about 100 of the ESA ladies to greet Danny upon his arrival.

He got off the plane and put on a little dog and pony show, you might say. He was acting like "I can't see," and he was holding on to the walls.

"I'm sick," he said. And the women just doted all over him. They were just thrilled to see Danny Thomas.

When we got back to the hotel room, I realized that he might not be putting on quite as much as I had originally thought. But he was here and that was what was important.

We had connecting suites, and we kept the door open, so we could talk while we were getting ready.

As we were changing into our tuxedoes, he was yelling at me, again, in that raspy low whisper, "I can't talk. You'd better be ready to go."

"All right," I said. "I'm ready, if something happens, I'll do my best. But there's only one Danny Thomas."

We went down stairs, and as we entered the banquet room, and were greeted by 3,000 ladies all dressed up in their most beautiful evening gowns.

They were clapping and whistling, hootin' and a hollerin'.

And honest to goodness, that's all it took to bring Danny back to life.

He stood up there and gave a wonderful, emotionally inspired talk about his promise; about helping the children; and doing God's work.

The talk was brilliant; it was reminiscent of the speech he gave in Houston. But what really impressed me that night, when I look back on how bad he was feeling, was his fortitude, his valor, and his mettle.

There's no other way to say it, "He was a true warrior for the cause."

And I felt so honored to serve under a leader like that.

He was always so selfless; he did it for the kids.

Saturday afternoon: The first thing on the ESA International agenda, the children of St. Jude.

They overwhelmingly adopted St. Jude as their national philanthropic project.

And what did that mean to us?

It was an incredible victory. It meant that over 30,000 women all across America were going to be raising money to help fight childhood cancer.

BOOK 4

The Memoirs of Jim Maloof

Book 4: Chapter 1: The Affiliate Opens

In 1972, the St. Jude Children's Research Hospital Midwest Affiliate Clinic opened with a good deal of fanfare.

After all, it was a historic moment for St. Jude and for Peoria, Illinois. The Midwest Affiliate Clinic was the first of its kind anywhere in the world.

All the local media showed up, as did several people from the national media.

There was food and live music; politicians were running around kissing babies; and balloons were floating up to the sky.

The Affiliate was located just inside the Methodist Hospital lobby, in a little 12' x 12' office. Granted, it wasn't much, but it was a start.

Clarence Yordy, Danny Thomas and myself, we all participated in the ribbon cutting ceremony. And what a wonderful, wonderful moment that was.

Mike Tamer and a whole bunch of other St. Jude guys were on hand to celebrate alongside many of my hometown friends.

Dr. Moris Adland and Dr. John Taraska were recognized for all their hard work. It was these two guys that basically helped launched the clinic, from a hands-on perspective.

All of the Methodist officials were there, as was Marge Crowl.

Without a doubt, the opening of the affiliate was an extra-special day for the patients living in this area. It meant receiving care here at home, instead of traveling to Memphis every time they needed a check-up, a blood transfusion, or treatment, or something like that.

From this day forward, the lives of families living in the Midwest were going to be changed, and those of us who had been involved for so long, knew it.

It was a very special day for me as well, and in more than just one way.

I was named "Founder of St. Jude Children's Research Hospital Midwest Affiliate Clinic" and elected Chairman of the Board of Directors for the Affiliate – a position I've never relinquished.

Really, it was a perfect day. The only thing missing from the celebration was my mother, but I knew she was smiling down on all of us.

I guess when I look back over my life, over the highs and lows, 1972 was a high point for me in terms of recognition.

Not only was I named "Founder" and "Chairman of the Board" of the Midwest Affiliate, but I also had the honor of being elected the Executive Vice-President of ALSAC National.

That was hard to believe. I could still remember, just like it was yesterday, telling old Nimer Haddad, "No, I don't want to go to your meeting in Chicago."

And now, here I was preparing to serve a two year term at the highest position one could be elected within ALSAC.

Of course, Danny Thomas was the one and only President of the ALSAC National Board of Directors: Danny's position being honorary.

So, the Executive Vice-President, that was it, the pinnacle, the culmination of 15 years hard work and dedication to the cause. But I didn't have time to enjoy the titles, with every title there was more work waiting to be done.

Down in Memphis, we broke ground on a newly planned seven-story tower. It would be the first thing that you'd see as you came across the bridge into Memphis. Emblazoned over the top, for everybody to see, like a beacon of hope spelled out in electric light, it would say "St. Jude Children's Research Hospital."

When it was completed it became the centralized research hub for St. Jude.

And no question about it Dr. Pinkel and the research staff needed more space. They had discovered better methods to diagnose. They had discovered the effectiveness of chemotherapy against certain types of cancer; and that chemotherapy and radiation can work together.

I saw the seven-story tower as a tribute, in effect, to the success of the doctors, nurses, and research specialists that were dedicating their lives to saving lives.

And as word of the hospital's success continued to spread, more families wanted to bring their children here – and to the Affiliate.

Family vacations and time together was getting harder. I was on the go all of the time and our children were all grown up now.

Our oldest son Michael was 30; Mark was 25; Nick, 21; and our baby daughter Janice was 19.

Wow. Where did the time go?

It seemed like just the other day when the whole family would climb in the car and head over to the Ein for dinner and a relaxing evening.

The Ein was located right next to Dixon's fish ponds on the Illinois River, right over there on state route 116.

A Lebanese guy by the name of Frank Zosky, a contractor, drew up the plans and the members built it.

Juta Etowah el Wadi, I think, was the Arabic name which translated into "The Place by the Water," but we nicknamed it *the Ein*, I was told, meant "clubhouse." It was the clubhouse of the ALSS (American Lebanese Syrian Society).

It was always such a cheerful place, with little children running all over; the smell of falafel; and the warmth of family and friends.

All the Lebanese people would get together. They'd do little skits up on the stage. The women would cook and sit around and talk, and the men would play pinnacle and sit around and talk.

You could never say enough about that place. It was a sacred place, it even had its own natural spring water that we pumped right out of the ground.

Oh, those were good times.

Also in the summer, Trudy and I would take the kids over to my brother Mitchell's house. Mitchell had an in-ground trampoline. Like an in-ground swimming pool, I kid you not, he dug a hole in the yard and sunk the trampoline down into it, and the kids played on that trampoline for hours on end.

I can't count the number of bones that were broken on that stupid thing. But the kids loved it.

Sometimes, we'd go fishing in Minnesota; sometimes, we'd stay home and fish on the river.

On of my favorite fishing companions was Louie Ayoub. Louie was one of the best human beings God ever created. He could make a seven course meal out of a couple of hot dogs. And he was a funny man too, once he put a 4' lamp in our fishing boat, I don't know why, but it was funny. You probably had to be there.

But as I'd drive from town to town, raising money for St. Jude, those were just some of the things I'd be thinking about.

Danny once told me that I was a better singer than he was. And that's always been a very private, very personal remembrance. It made me feel warm inside: it made me feel like God had given me a special gift. And sometimes I'd think about that too as I drove around from town to town singing to the song on the radio.

Book 4: Chapter 4: Tragedy

One day, late in 1973, Trudy and I came home from an evening out, when eerily we found our son Mark in the basement. He had tried to commit suicide.

LORD HAVE MERCY!

We cut him down from the rafters and rushed him to the hospital.

Thank God he was alive.

He couldn't tell us what was wrong. We didn't know either. But we knew for sure he needed help. We took him to all kinds of doctors, who referred us to all kinds of specialist.

At the time, we didn't know he would make other attempts. The doctor's tried their best to help him, they even tried shock therapy. It was horrible.

It was a trying time for the entire family.

"Lord," I prayed, "help our son."

Mike Tamer was the lion, the leader, the catalyst behind ALSAC. He molded that organization in his own image, in his own self-determined image.

He was the one and only National Executive Director of Fundraising for ALSAC, a position he held since day one.

And on November 13, 1974, the lion laid down: Mike Tamer passed away.

I sang at his funeral in Indianapolis, and Danny did the Eulogy. It was a very difficult time, both, for me and for the organization.

After Mike Tamer's death, Danny and Rose Marie Thomas invited Trudy and I out to California on two different occasions.

They flew us out there trying to persuade me to take over the job as fundraising executive director for the nation.

The job would require moving to Indianapolis, because that's where the fundraising headquarters was located.

It was an amazing opportunity. A once in a lifetime opportunity, but we couldn't go. There was absolutely no way.

Our son and our family needed us here.

Despite our best efforts and the efforts of the doctors, our son was not making progress. He had since made attempts on his own life.

And on June 22, 1975, our son Mark lost his battle with depression. He committed suicide by asphyxiation at our home. He was 27, not yet even in the prime of his life. He could have gone on to become a marvelous pianist, but the good Lord took him.

And like many families, we'd say, "Why me, God? Why us?"

It's heartbreaking, even today.

Within a year the Affiliate had outgrown its original space, and Methodist moved us up to a specially designated area on the 4th floor.

By 1975, Methodist gave us a whole wing on the 5th floor. I don't remember how many square feet or how many rooms, but it was a major move.

The hospital did something like $20 million dollars in expansion during this time. And they were always looking out for us, making sure we had the best of everything.

They had such a wonderful faith in what we were doing.

When the doors first opened, nineteen patients began their treatments at the Midwest Affiliate, and that number just keeps growing and growing.

St. Jude was rapidly expanding and rapidly changing; and not just the Affiliate, but in Memphis too.

For instance, Dr. Pinkel, the first and only director of St. Jude Children's Research Hospital, had retired at the end of 1973, and Dr. Alvin Mauer was now in charge of day-to-day operations.

Mike Tamer's position was filled temporarily by Fred Gattas, Sr., while the search for a new leader continued.

Tamer ran his show out of Indianapolis, because that's where he was from. But now Gattas, serving in the interim, made the bold decision to move the ALSAC Headquarters to Memphis – a move which was controversial at the time, but one I fully supported.

Eventually, Baddia "Bud" Rashid was brought in to take over Tamer's job. Rashid had worked for the Justice Department, so he brought excellent legal and administrative skills to the position.

But since nobody –not me, not Bud, nobody– could fill Tamer's shoes, the Board of Directors agreed to hire Rashid some extra help.

There's nothing that's not been done under the sun, and there's no use re-inventing the wheel.

Jerry Lewis was raising crazy amounts of money with his Muscular Dystrophy telethons. For several years now, he'd gone over the $10 million dollar mark. Wow.

In 1977, Danny Thomas launched a localized telethon in Los Angeles which brought in over a quarter of a million dollars for St. Jude.

As the Chairman of the Board for the St. Jude Midwest Affiliate, I knew we had to do more than we were currently doing if we wanted our clinic to grow.

To me, a local telethon seemed like a possible answer?

And if I was right, the questions were "How do I go about putting it together?" "Who do I call?" And, "What do we need?"

If you remember, it took me a week to convince Bergner's President Tom Listen to give me 100 shopping bags for the first Teen March: lousy shopping bags probably didn't even cost a nickel a piece.

Tom and I were buddies, and we used to talk to each other like that all of the time. And I never missed an opportunity to kid him about those bags.

And in return he'd say to me, "All right you dirty old A-rab, quite fooling around with me with this penny ante stuff, shopping bags, $500 bucks. Give me something big, a project that Bergner's can really wrap their arms around."

Early in 1978, I told him, "Tom, I think I'm going to have something for you. Let me talk to a few people first, and then I'll get back to you. But if I can pull it together, you're going to like it, a lot."

I turned to my good friend Bill Adams, the General Manager at WEEK-TV.

I said, "Bill, St. Jude is growing. The Affiliate is growing and we need to raise some money locally, how about a telethon?"

"No, we can't do that," he said.

"What do you mean, 'we can't do that'?"

"It's company policy Jim. We don't do them, not for you, not for anybody."

I said, "Come on Bill, this is St. Jude. We don't take 'no' for an answer. Why don't you go to the next board meeting and make a strong appeal about how we are raising money for sick children. You do that for me, and I'll line up a couple of sponsors for you."

"I don't think I can do that."

"Bill Adams, don't look at me and say you can't. Say, 'I'll try.' Say, 'I'll try' and I'll leave you alone."

"Alright, I'll try, but I'm not promising anything."

A month later, Bill went to a board meeting to talk to the owners of the company in Kansas City.

He took my challenge and went directly to them. He convinced them that they should try it for one year.

And just like that, he had changed corporate policy. Who says what's done can't be undone?

They not only allowed it, but Bill Adams, God Bless Bill, he got them to underwrite the entire cost of the telethon: all of the production costs.

And this wasn't just a little penny-ante event. It was going to be from 6:30 p.m. to 12:30 a.m. No commercials, no newsbreaks, nothing except a St. Jude Telethon.

Wow. I was almost speechless, when Bill told me all this.

I took that news and went right up to Tom Liston's office.

"Okay, you old windbag, you've been preaching to me for years about wanting something big. Are you ready for this?" And I told him everything.

He didn't bat an eye.

He said, "You've got it. Now you're talking. Bergner's wants to be a part of that. We love this community; we love St. Jude; and we want to be a part of that. So, yes, you have a sponsor."

The first St. Jude telethon on WEEK-TV was set for the first weekend in August.

WEEK-TV weatherman Vic Burnett was my brave and dutiful co-host. It was just the two of us. We'd never done anything like this before, and honestly, we got by on a wing and a prayer.

The telethon was held in the WEEK studios over in East Peoria.

Bergner's also provided the telephones. And as chairman of the event, I helped round up volunteers to answer those phones.

We raised $90,000 dollars that first telethon.

What a start, it was good.

But what I remember more than anything else, the response from the community was overwhelming. The number of people calling in and making pledges, the number of people who wrote letters and mailed in checks was just unbelievable.

The response was so positive that WEEK decided to do it for a second year, and then beyond.

Every once in a while, Danny would call me up and ask, "How the heck are you raising all that money in that little cow town?"

The answer was simple, I wasn't doing it, the community was doing it.

One example would be Peoria's first St. Jude Golf Classic.

In the spring of 1980, I was playing golf with Dave Ryan and Ernie Horvath out at Mount Hawley Country Club.

Dave and Ernie were the owners of Dave and Ernie's Lums over on Knoxville. They were real characters and everybody liked them, and their restaurant was popular too.

So, one day out on the green, I said to them, "I don't think anyone, at least to my knowledge, has a worthwhile golf tournament. You guys ought to put on a golf tournament for St. Jude."

They said, "How are we going to do that?"

"You guys are successful at everything you do, you don't need to ask me how to do it, just do it."

A few days later, they saw me, and they were all excited.

"Hey, Jim. We are going to do the golf tournament."

"Great! When?" I asked. "Next Year?"

"No," they said, "we are going to do it in June."

"June?"

"Yeah."

I could hardly believe they had enough time to organize the thing, June was just a month away.

We hit up another friend of ours, Fred Jacobs for some help.

Fred was a Caterpillar mid-management executive, a true bean counter. He was also my accountant, at Jim Maloof Realty.

He came up with a layout, or plan, of how a golf tournament should be organized and run. And his plan was so well conceived that the people in Memphis asked him to come down and speak to their fundraising committee officers about it.

And he did. And Peoria's golf event was used as a model throughout the nation for literally dozens or maybe hundreds of golf events around the country.

Our St. Jude Golf Tournament, by the way, raised $24,000 dollars that first year.

In 1982, momentum was picking up. I was playing golf with another friend of mine, Hiles Stout.

Hiles was well-known in the community. He had been an all-state everything athlete for Central High School back in the day.

Basketball, football, Hiles played them all.

But now he and his wife were heavy into tennis.

So, one night out at Mount Hawley, sitting down on one of the fairways, I said to him, "Hiles, wouldn't it be great if we had a tennis tournament? We have a golf classic, why don't we have a tennis classic?"

Like I had heard so many times before, he said, "Well, I don't know if we can do that."

"Hiles," I said, like I said to others before him, "don't tell me 'we can't do that.' Tell me you'll try."

And that same year, there was a tennis classic to raise money for St. Jude.

Book 4: Chapter 10: Memphis to Peoria Run

Perhaps the most incredible local St. Jude fundraising event was spawned in 1981, when Michael McCoy and a young man by the name of Gene Pratt accepted my challenge of putting together a small run out at Landmark, the fitness center.

They did it, and I don't know they raised a few hundred bucks or something that year.

But they came back to me all excited and said, "Guess what?"

And naturally I said, "What? What do you boys want now?"

"We are going to have a run."

And I said, "Oh, okay, another one."

"No. No," they said, "not at Landmark. We are going to get the runners to run from Memphis to Peoria."

"You must be out of your cotton-pickin' mind. Who the hell can ever do that?"

"You'll see," they said. "We're going to drive a bunch of runners down to Memphis in motor homes, stay the night, then we'll turn around and run all the way back to Peoria arriving at the telethon on Saturday night."

"I'll believe it, when I see it," I said. I've got to tell you, they sounded like a couple of screwballs to me.

A couple of weeks passed and I hadn't heard anything from either one. I wasn't necessarily surprised.

I found the rest of this out later, but I guess they had a meeting and decided to advertise for runners; and that didn't work out so well. They also went to cities outside of Peoria, trying to recruit runners, but weren't too successful there either. So, finally, they decided that perhaps they would wait another year.

They had also decided, the next one to see Jim Maloof would be the one to tell him they were going to postpone the run until the following year.

Now, as the Good Lord would have it, Trudy and I were over at Landmark for some sort of luncheon. And wouldn't you know it, the first person we ran into was Mike McCoy.

So, I approached him. "Alright Mike, how's the run going?"

"Oh fine, we are moving right ahead. It'll be a good one," he said.

Mike saw Gene later on that same day.

"I ran into Jim Maloof," he told Gene.

"Oh, good, you told him the news."

"Yeah," Michael said, "yeah. We are going to do the run."

"What?"

"I told Jim, 'it's coming along well.'"

Apparently, Michael was afraid to tell me they were going to wait until next year. And I don't know if Gene

Pratt was about to have a conniption or whatever, but anyhow, they did do the run that first year.

And the first Memphis to Peoria run had 22 runners and they raised $22,000 dollars.

And, just like they promised, they arrived at the telethon on that Saturday night.

I tell you, you never saw a group of guys and gals that looked so tired. I think they said, twice, they were about ready to fold it up and drive home.

Tired and beat they might have been, but their small victory was the start of a wonderful, symbolic, enduring, and growing tradition.

Amy McClellan was a cute little kid from Morton, Illinois.

She'd been off treatment for about 8 or 9 years. And just as she was told that she was about to be permanently cured –she had a relapse and went back in the hospital.

When you have a relapse, sometimes, in fact, a lot of times, it's more serious than the first.

It's absolutely devastating news. It creates tears of despair, and threatens to wipe out all the hope that has been built up.

I remember visiting her mom at the hospital until maybe 1 or 2 o'clock in the morning. And finally, I asked her, knowing that they were not Catholic, if she'd consider wearing my St. Jude medal until Amy got better.

And she agreed.

There's always been something special about that medal. Danny gave it to me the second time we met, and I've been wearing it ever since.

And so, I offered it to Amy's mom, as I had done with other parents at different times.

And she wore it faithfully, until she didn't need to wear it anymore.

Amy got well.

She went to Knox College where she became an

honors student.

She grew into a beautiful, beautiful young lady and went on to become Miss Heart of Illinois.

She became a teacher.

And, as a testament to her faith in St. Jude, she even became a St. Jude Runner, raising money for other young kids.

Eventually, she got married to a young man by the name of Ryan Jones, and today, they've got a lovely baby girl.

I sang at their wedding, and, wow, let me tell you, that was a real tear-jerker for me.

Over the years we've had a few celebrities drop in on our telethon.

Perhaps the biggest of all was when Mr. Las Vegas himself, Wayne Newton, stopped in to visit us one night. "Danke Schoen," Mr. Wayne Newton.

Naturally, Danny Thomas made his way onto our telethon a couple of times. And his adorable daughter Marlo Thomas came to see us one year. Many of you will remember Marlo for her role in the '60's hit television show *That Girl* – and maybe the fact that she married Emmy winning talk show host, Phil Donahue. She's also the National Outreach Director for St. Jude, a post she's held for many, many, years now.

Another one of my favorite moments was when actress Ann Jillian stopped by the telethon. Jillian had been a big television star in the '80's, when at 35-years old she was diagnosed with cancer.

Her battle and triumph were made into a made-for-TV movie called *The Ann Jillian Story*. It was quite a story, and she is quite an amazing lady.

But what a lot of people didn't know about Ann was that she had a remarkable singing voice. And I got to sing with her when she visited our telethon. That was a real honor.

Shortly afterwards, Ann invited Trudy and I up to see her perform at the Drury Lane Theatre in Chicago.

Ann knew which night we'd be there, and that night, she pulled me out of the audience and had me sing a duet with her. It came as a total surprise to me, I had no idea it was going to happen. We actually sang three numbers in all. And what a thrill it was for this old guy from Peoria, let me tell you.

Little Billy Johnson had grown up. It had been many years since his days at the Peoria State Hospital.

He had lived with a friend out in the Washington, D.C. area. And then moved to Mountainside Hospital near Montclair, New Jersey, which was straight down the I-95 corridor to D.C.

Billy had heard that Danny was coming to Washington to speak at a symposium held at the historic Sheraton Washington Hotel.

So, he called me in Peoria.

"I've got to meet Danny again," he told me. "I've just got to meet Danny again."

"Why Billy?"

"I've got a—another surprise for him. You're going to l-l-love it."

"Okay, Billy, let me see what I can do. Let me get back to you."

I called Danny and told him of Billy's request.

Danny said, "Fine, no problem, if that's what he wants. We did well last time listening to the young man. We are going to listen to him again."

And when I arrived in Washington, D.C., there was my old friend Billy Johnson waiting for me.

That evening Danny was the featured speaker at this sort-of question-and-answer style conference or symposium.

There where about 1,000 people gathered to talk about St. Jude and to also raise some money.

The place was absolutely beautiful, inside and out.

When Danny was introduced, he approached the podium, made some welcoming remarks and then said, "Now, Jim Maloof, I understand we have a special guest in the audience."

I stood up; helped Billy up; and I escorted him to the podium.

Oh, they hugged and all of that stuff.

Danny quickly told Billy's story. And Billy stood there, right next to him, bobbing his head up and down in agreement with everything Danny said.

At the conclusion of the story, Danny said, "Billy, I understand that you have another surprise for me?"

"I-I-I do have," he said.

And again, Billy clutched a white envelope in his trembling, palsied hand. But, this time the white envelope did not jingle. It did not have the sound of any coins in it.

"When I heard you were coming to Washington, I asked Jim Maloof if I could meet you and show you what I've been doing."

"Can you tell me, what's in the envelope Billy?"

"The last time we met, I gave you 75 cents. Now I have been saving my one dollar bills. And I know that it cost a lot of money to run that hospital today. And this time, I have saved for you $75 dollars."

Needless-to-say, the place broke up.

Danny got all teary-eyed, well, not bawling like the first time, but he was touched, you could tell.

And then he really made a big fuss about the fact that if this young man could save $75 dollars, why can't you open up your pocketbook and give something to this great cause and help fight childhood cancer.

It was just another of those great moments in the history of St. Jude, and there's been so many.

Another was in 1985, when President Ronald Reagan awarded Danny Thomas with the Congressional Gold Medal in honor of all the work he had done on behalf of St. Jude.

And I was there.

Book 4: Chapter 15: The New Atrium Building

Methodist was once again growing.

In 1991, they constructed the beautiful Atrium Building down on corner of NE Glen Oak Avenue and Main Street, right at the bottom of Main Street hill.

The Atrium Building is maybe 7 or 8 stories tall, and houses all kinds of offices and facilities for the medical community.

It has a Wellness Center in it, with a gym and pool, and classes on nutrition, all kinds of stuff.

There's every kind of specialist you could think of housed in there, from diabetes to gastrointestinal. They got it all.

Anyway, Methodist was expanding, and the Midwest Affiliate was expanding too.

In fact, St. Jude had grown to the point where Methodist moved us out of the main hospital and into the new Atrium Building. And we were given half a floor there.

Board members, the national board members, came up from Memphis and had one of their meetings here. They were just thrilled, absolutely thrilled, to see how far we had come since we started in that little 12' x 12' back in 1972.

The Next Jim Maloof

The survival rate at St. Jude was now close to 70%, which was a far cry from 4% when we started.

But unfortunately, there was still that 30%. And one of those youngsters was my friend Dusty Paulter.

Dusty was from Dunlap, Illinois. He got straight A's, was on the student council, and played in the school honors band.

He was brilliant, absolutely brilliant.

If Dusty had not of lost his battle with leukemia, I honestly believe, he would have gone on to become the next St. Jude spokesman. He just had that kind of sparkle and passion in his personality.

When he passed away, I did the eulogy at his funeral and I sang the song *On Eagles Wings*.

Whenever we lose a child at St. Jude it is difficult. But for me Dusty was one of the most difficult, because he had so much to offer the world. And he was only 12-years old.

Since then, I am proud to say, his entire family is carrying on his legacy.

His dad, Kevin, is currently the President of the Midwest Affiliate and doing a wonderful job at it as well.

His mom, Joy, is a telethon volunteer, and a year-round fundraiser. She's always cooking some fundraiser up, be it a pork chop or spaghetti dinner.

And Dusty's sister, Jeri, wasn't even 2-years old when he died, but she does a little bit of everything to help raise money for St. Jude. She recently made the Memphis to Peoria run.

The entire family keeps Dusty's memory alive by staying involved. They are such warm, compassionate, and loving people.

Their dedication to the cause is an inspiration to so many other families out there, because they are leading by example. They have been through the fire and have come out stronger and more determined than ever to defeat childhood cancer.

Book 4: Chapter 17: **Six Days Later**

Only six days after the death of Dusty Paulter, my good friend Danny Thomas died. He had a heart attack on February 6, 1991.

Lord have mercy!

Talk about a heartbreaking week. It was just terrible.

I had just talked to Danny about ten days before.

I remember we were trying to set up a date when he might be able to come to Peoria for the formal dedication of our new St. Jude facility – which was now in the Artium Building.

He said he was feeling great. He said he was looking forward to finalizing a date and coming back to Peoria.

He sounded fabulous. So, yeah, I was shocked.

I was an honorary pall bearer for Danny's funeral in Los Angeles.

You know, every time Danny heard about a child dying of cancer, he took it very hard. He felt it was unacceptable and it made him work that much harder for St. Jude.

Book 4: Chapter 18: What One Person Can Do

Bob Jockisch was a back up defensive tackle for the fighting Irish of Notre Dame in the late 1960's. He graduated in '68, one year before Joe Thiesmann would lead the team to their first bowl game in almost 50 years.

After college Bob came back to Peoria and worked for RJ Distributing Co.

Eventually, he became a distributor for Coors, and a friend, a good friend, of Peter Coors, the owner of Coors Brewery in Denver.

I had come to know Bob through his involvement with civic organizations within the community here in Peoria. And over the years, we too became good friends.

Bob, on his own initiative convinced Peter Coors to come to Peoria to see the affiliate. Peter Coors came and he was so moved by what he saw that he promised that St. Jude would be the number 1 charity for Coors nationally.

And from that humble little beginning here in Peoria, the Peoria connection as I like to say, they have raised over $30 million dollars and are still going strong.

And that's proof of what one person can do.

That same year, in '95, Memphis announced that the Peoria affiliate would now be used as a model for other affiliates around the country.

And, a little side note, keep this in mind for a little later, the NBA introduced two new teams into the league that year, the Toronto Raptors and the Vancouver Grizzlies, as a part of their expansion into Canada.

Twice I was a survivor in business: first in the 60's and then in the '80's.

I was in real estate now, but those were tough times '80, '81, '82, and '83. There were over 5,000 houses available on the market. And I couldn't sell or rent a one of them.

The business was barely surviving. It was just horrible. Just to keep afloat we had to keep borrowing and borrowing money to the point where the bank said, "We like you. We think this is a great opportunity, but we can't keep lending you money."

And two days before Christmas, Christmas was on a Sunday, so this was on a Friday, in 1983, when I get a call early in the morning from my attorney Tim Howard.

"What are you doing?"

"This is the last day for shopping and I've got to buy something for Trudy."

He said, "I've got to see you today."

"I'm not going to be around today, can't it wait?"

"Jim," he said, "I've got to see you right away."

"But Tim, I have got to go get these gifts before the stores close."

"It'll only take a few minutes. You stay there and I will be right out."

I didn't like it, but he was so insistant. So, I said, "Okay, come on over."

In the meantime, I spend a little time going over my Christmas list. And then, about noon, he arrives and gives me the news.

Tim, by the way, was also the attorney for Commercial Bank. And so he says to me, "Jim, this is one of the hardest things I have ever had to do in my entire legal life. It's hard because we're such good friends. But the bank is going to close you down."

"They can't do that," I said. "What do they want?"

"I hate to even say it, but they want $83,000 dollars by this coming Wednesday."

"Wait a minute," I said. "Are you kidding me? Don't you know that Christmas is Sunday? Can't I get some time, an extension or something? I mean that's only a few days."

With a heavy heart, I went out and bought all my Christmas presents. And needless to say, I bought a few less then I had planned on buying.

I returned home about 4 p.m.

As I walked in, Trudy said, "What's that look on your face?"

"I got some bad news today, but I'll tell you about it a bit later."

I sat in my little office thinking, "Where am I going to get $83,000 dollars from?"

It's now after 5 o'clock. All the stores are closed, the banks are closed. Where do you get $83,000 dollars on a Friday night on a holiday weekend? You don't.

Who could possibly help me? I wondered.

I started thumbing through my little black book, and that's when I stumbled across Danny Thomas's number.

Hum? I knew the chances of him picking up the phone were only about 1 in 1,000, but what did I have to lose?

I picked up the phone and dialed the number. And, lo and behold, he picked it up: that in and of itself was a miracle.

I told him my problem and the first words out of his mouth were "Don't worry about it."

"What do you mean, 'Don't worry about it'? Come Thursday, I'll be out of business."

"No, you won't be out of business," he said. "You've been helping St. Jude out for a long time now. And now it's our turn to help you. Do you have a board of director's list?"

"Yeah, I've got one."

"Half of them," he said, "are very wealthy. Let's pick out 12 or 13 names. I'll call half and you'll call half. I'll tell my list and you tell your list your problem."

"Danny are you sure?"

"Of course," he said with all of the confidence I was lacking. "And another thing, tell them that I'm going to give you $20,000 dollars to start it off."

"What?"

"And if we need more, I'll be there," he said. "Now, let's get calling."

I started calling and it wasn't just luck that I

caught every single one of them at home. I felt the presence of the Lord with me.

Everyone I talked to said the same thing, "Don't tell me why you need it, just tell me what you need."

And so $5,000 dollars from this one, $3,000 dollars from that one, and $7,000 dollars from another one.

Periodically, Danny would call back and say, "How are you doing? How are you doing?"

"Hey, I'm batting 100%."

Then he said, "Fine, put me down for another $5,000 dollars. And tell your people I'm giving you $25,000 dollars."

I asked him how he was doing and he said, "Don't you worry about that. I'll have the money there."

And within an hour or so we had raised close to $90,000.

That money was overnighted and on my desk by Wednesday afternoon. Some of it arrived as early as Tuesday, and I could tell the bank I was halfway there.

And as crazy as it sounds, that's how I became a two-time survivor in business.

They all got paid back. Not one of them wanted interest on their loan.

"You don't worry about interest," they said. "Just pay me back when you can. I don't care whether it's $10 or $100 or $1,000 dollars at a time. Just pay me back when you get it."

And that was the way it was with all of them.

And out of all of that, I found another reason to believe that there is someone much stronger and greater than us all. Yes, I believe that God made it all possible, not just once, but twice.

BOOK 5

The Memoirs of Jim Maloof

Book 5: Chapter 1: The Decision to Run for Mayor

Early on Thanksgiving Day, 1984, I was downstairs in the kitchen preparing the family holiday dinner.

As tradition would have it, the family always came to our house: our oldest son Michael and his family would be coming; as would our son Nick and his wife and kids; and our daughter Janice and her friend from church.

They would all be arriving in another five or six hours, and I wanted everything to be just right.

About 7:30 a.m. Trudy came downstairs.

"Oh, the turkey smells good."

"Happy Thanksgiving," I said. "Guess what?"

"What do you mean, 'Guess what?'"

She walked right over to me and gave me the once over. "I don't like the look on your face," she said.

"Well, you're not going to like it any better when I get done."

Her morning smile had turned into a more serious look of apprehension. She didn't respond, she just looked at me and waited for the news.

"I just decided, I'm going to run for mayor."

"Mayor of what?"

"Mayor of Peoria."

"You can't even pay the bills for your business. You're lucky you've still got the doors open. And you want to tell me that you want to be the mayor of this town?"

"Yeah."

"Who told you to do it? Who asked you?"

"Nobody asked me. I haven't talked to a single person."

It was true, nobody had asked me. It was a decision I made based on what I saw going on all around me.

Times were bad. There were a lot of good, decent, hard-working people standing in food lines. Unemployment had hit 18%; 30,000 people were out of work at Caterpillar; and there were over 5,000 homes on the market, and I couldn't sell or rent a one of them.

People would say to me, "Jim, you were so good to us when we bought our home, you helped us out, but my husband and I can't find work, so we're moving out of town. Here's the keys to our house. It's yours, take over the mortgage and it's yours."

"Whoa, whoa, whoa! Wait a minute now, I can't sell it. I can't rent it. What am I going to do with it? Just pay mortgages?"

Anyway, I looked Trudy square in the eyes and said, "Trudy, girl, I don't know. I really don't know. I'm saying to you, for the first time, that's what's in my heart right now. I'm telling you that I am going to run for mayor. Somebody has got to help straighten this town up. Somebody has to help the people."

"Oh, you crazy man!"

She knew that if I said it and meant it, that's probably what I would do.

And this old crazy man said it and meant it, and that's probably what I would do.

She came closer and gave me a hug, and her smile returned. "Okay," she said, "you know I'll be right there with you."

She was pure gold.

Book 5: Chapter 2: No Political Experience?

It was true, I had no political experience. As a young man I'd been involved in the Junior Chamber of Commerce, and I had done a little lobbying to help get the crooks out of Peoria back in the late '40's and early '50's, but I never held any office or anything like that. In fact, the closest I came to politics is when I sat on the board of the Peoria Civic Center Commission.

And let me remind you, in the late 1970's the Civic Center was a hot topic; it darn near created a civil war in Peoria.

And how did I get involved?

That was another civil war. Back in '73, I backed Dick Carver for mayor. Not such a big deal, right.

Well, my brother Mitchell decided to toss his hat in the ring and run for mayor as well.

I didn't change my allegiance, I continued to back Carver. Now this wasn't to spite my brother or anything of the kind. In fact, my brother Mitchell and I have always had a pretty good relationship.

But at the time, I just felt like Carver was the person who could best help our community.

And I've always felt that way. I like to say, "It's not who I'm for, it's what I'm for."

I never pick a candidate by the party they belong to, or the friendship you have with them or the relation they are to you. When I back a candidate, I do so because I believe they will be the person who can best help our community.

Even though I'm a Republican, I've put my support behind some good people over the years, people who've happened to be Democrats, like State's Attorney Kevin Lyons and Senator George Shadid.

And they've gone on to do some very good things.

And yes, that's the same George Shadid that drove Danny and I over to the Peoria State Hospital when we first met Billy Johnson.

Anyway, the point being, I had supported Carver in his election and re-election as mayor.

So we got to know each other; we liked each other; and when he started selecting people to sit on the newly formed Peoria Civic Center Commission, in the late '70's, he asked me.

And I said, "Yes."

I was for building a civic center, even before Carver asked me to be on the board. I was for it because those who came up with the idea, and then the plan to implement it, had a vision of what it might mean for the community. How it could enhance the image of the community. And they had long-term vision, which I thought was important.

I was elected secretary of the commission and sat on the planning and design committee.

As part of my job, I used to go to neighborhood meetings and field questions from people.

Go Help the Children & God Help You

People from every walk of life, from every neighborhood in Peoria, they were all afraid that we were going to tax them to death in order to pay for the new $64 million dollar civic center.

When these naysayers would come to our neighborhood meetings, they would attack our plan.

So, I'd get up, point my finger at them and say, "You've got to have courage and the nerve to do what is good for the community."

Oh, they'd boo me, and heckle me. Let me tell you, the people against the civic center were intense and passionate. Sometimes, there'd be so much hissing and whatnot, nobody could hear anybody else. Sometimes, these meetings would just turn into chaos.

But when they'd finally let me finish, then I'd say, "There will be no taxes paid by the people."

The people for the civic center would clap and cheer real loud.

Then, of course, on the other side, they'd whine and complain and say, "Sixty million dollars, somebody's paying for it, and it's going to be us."

But that wasn't the case, not at all. There was a promise then, and it is still this way today, that says that the Peoria Civic Center would be paid for out of our hotel, restaurant, and amusement taxes (HRA).

So, I'd explain it to them, "What happens is that all of the visitors, all of the people from the surrounding areas, all of the people who spend money in the local hotels, in the local restaurants, and in the local theaters, will pay a 3% tax on those items. And that is where the money comes from to pay for the civic center.

"And, thanks to the hard work and efforts of Fred Tuerk and Senator Prescott Bloom, we've already received a $20 million dollar grant from the state of Illinois.

"So, that leaves us with balance of $44 million dollars, which will then be paid through the HRA taxes."

It was my job to try to explain this over and over again at meeting after meeting.

People didn't understand it, or didn't want to believe it, I'm not sure which.

Sharing some of these meeting with me were members of the Peoria City Council, there were 9 of them, including Mayor Carver. Generally, they were all seated at a long conference table, and I would point my finger at each and every one of them, reminding them of their responsibility to the community.

I would remind them that the civic center was not so much for them, but for their children and their children's children, and for the enjoyment and enrichment of the people that would one day be coming to this community.

And naturally, the audience would react appropriately if they were for or against it.

While all that was going on, I quietly continued building up my real estate business and singing in my free time.

The civic center was never put to a referendum. A referendum is when, at some particular election time, the people can vote their opinion "for" or "against."

If the civic center had been taken to a referendum, I have no doubt that it would have been defeated.

How did they avoid the referendum process? To this day, I still don't know. The whole thing was left in the hands of the Peoria City Council.

And, so, on the night they took their preliminary vote, the result was 5 to 4, with the "nays" coming out on top.

I always found it ironic, that my good friend, Dick Carver, originally voted against it. A lot of people don't know that. On the first vote, he voted against it. But when the final vote came down, he did vote for it: he voted for it the second time around.

I guess I was surprised that he originally voted against it, because he had worked so hard for it.

And even after he had voted against it, they still named the Carver arena after him – for his efforts to bring the civic center to Peoria. I guess that kind of surprised me too.

There was a lot of question about that, but I'm happy for Dick; he served eleven years as the Mayor and did an outstanding job.

Dick Carver, unbeknownst to a lot of people, was

also responsible for making the land available for the University of Illinois College of Medicine at Peoria, which sits across the street from Methodist's Atrium Building.

It was he that proposed the buyout of all the homes there at the foot of Main Street hill. And the city went ahead and bought those homes to open up that land for the College of Medicine. And the city also helped those people move.

But as the rest of Southtown, it was left a disaster. Absolutely, a disaster.

Book 5: Chapter 4: Carver Gets Nod By Reagan

In August of 1984, President Ronald Reagan hand picked Peoria Mayor Richard Carver to fill the recently vacated post of Assistant Secretary of the Air Force for the Department of Defense.

Dick was still an acting lieutenant colonel in the Air Force Reserves. Naturally, he accepted President Reagan's offer. Which was understandable, he was a three-term mayor. And he had done more than his share for this community. And again, we were all very happy for him.

To his credit goes the completion of the Peoria Civic Center with its theatre, arena, and exhibition hall.

The Civic Center, by the way, was actually designed by an internationally renowned architect; I think his name was Philip Johnson, if I remember that right.

Anyway, the economic downturn Peoria was soon to face started on Carver's watch as well, although I can't say it was his fault at all.

The closing of Hiram Walker in 1981, the last great vestige of Peoria's famous past as a distilling town, gave us only a small hint of what was to come. Then Pabst would close its doors only a few months later.

The entire nation was headed toward a major economic downturn, which would lead us into a major recession. And eventually lead me to make the decision to run for mayor.

My First Campaign Promise

When I officially decided to run for mayor, my first campaign promise was to do something about the 900-plus families that remained in Southtown.

If you remember, the Carver administration had already bought up the homes at the foot of Main Street hill. The Southtown area we are talking about here is between Dr. Martin Luther King Jr. Drive and SW Jefferson Avenue.

The living conditions were abominable. These people were living in the worst squalor you could ever imagine. Their homes were rat-infested, mice-infested, and falling down. You'd be afraid to walk into some of those homes. It was frightening.

Now the original intention was for the city to buy these homes. But with a nationwide recession, the city was standing still.

Nonetheless, the city kept advising the people living there – "do not improve your homes."

And so people did not improve their homes. Three or four years passed and the economy was waning, getting worse.

And so my first campaign promise was to move the people out of Southtown and into better housing and living conditions.

Book 5: Chapter 6: **Early Days of the Campaign**

In the early days of my campaign, I'd hold a press conference and the only two people who'd be there were me and Terry Towery of the *Peoria Journal Star.*

And Towery only showed up because he was new on the job, he probably would have shown up to watch paint dry if the *Journal Star* would have told him to.

Like the media, most of the general public was also taking my bid for mayor with a grain of salt.

But I kept plucking away. Every chance I'd get I'd make a small speech, Lion's Club, Elk's Club, it didn't matter. Wherever I could, I tried to let people know that I was serious.

And I didn't have much time, it was only three months from the time I decide to run until the Consolidated Primary Election, which was to be held on February 26, 1985.

There were four of us running in that Primary Election, and the clear front runner was Dan Gura.

Dan was a sitting Peoria City Councilman, so he had six years of experience behind him. And he was no dummy, he was the alumni and parent relations director over at Bradley University: he was a real smart and personable kind of guy.

He was the older brother of Tim Gura. Tim, if you remember, was the young man who rounded up all of those high school students for our first Teen March.

The Maloof family and the Gura family knew each other very well. Tim had been friends with our son Mark; Dan's wife and our daughter, Janice, were classmates and great friends; and Dan had actually worked for me out at the real estate company.

I liked Dan, but I felt the good Lord chose to have me run against him.

Shortly after I told Trudy of my decision to run, I picked up the phone.

"Happy Thanksgiving Dan. Guess what?"

"Why are you running? You don't have any experience." That's what he said.

I just told him, "I don't want you finding out through the grape vine. I thought you ought to hear it straight from me."

And so it was in the primary election in February of 1985 that Dan Gura walloped all 4 of us.

Walloped, that might even be an understatement. He whipped our hides but good.

I ran second however, which allowed me to run again in the general election in April.

Don Hickey, The Hoosier

And so it was right after the primary that a graduate student at Bradley University by the name of Don Hickey came to me and said, "Jim, do you really want to be mayor?"

I just had my butt kicked, you know, Dan Gura had won 113 or 114 out of the 120 precincts. It was Gura across the board. But I didn't want to give this young Indiana boy, this Hoosier, even the slightest hint of weakness. So with all the confidence I could muster, I said, "Certainly, I am not in this for second place."

He said, "Well, I think I've got your answer."

"What's that?"

"Do you know a man named Henry Cisneros?"

"I think he's the mayor somewhere down in Texas."

He said, "You're right, San Antonio. And he's got a program down there, and if you can get him to share his program with you, you will be the next mayor of Peoria."

"Why do you say that?"

"Because San Antonio, although a much larger city, had the same problem that Peoria has, but he put together this program, he called it Target 90's, and he resurrected his city with that program."

"How do I find him?"

"I don't know," Don said, "but you might want to start making some phone calls."

Early the next morning, I was calling information

trying to find this Henry Cisneros, the Mayor of San Antonio, Texas.

His name wasn't listed.

So I tried calling the San Antonio police station, but they wouldn't give his number.

I tried the head of the Chamber of Commerce, but they wouldn't give me his number.

I tried the city manager, some of the council people, and all that, but nobody would give me his number.

Then, as the Good Lord would have it, somebody leaked.

"Now, don't tell him where you got it," they said, "but here's the number."

Book 5: Chapter 8: Henry Cisneros

It was about 8:30 p.m. when I called the number I had been given.

"This is the residence of Henry Cisneros. May I help you?"

Holy cow! They had given me the mayor's home phone number.

And it was Henry Cisneros on the other end. Oh my goodness. I never thought I'd get him.

I introduced myself as an "old" 65-year-old guy that had never held office before, but that was running for mayor.

"I've heard about your program Target 90's," I said, "and I was wondering if you would share some thoughts on that with me?"

He was so impressed that a 65-year-old was running for mayor that he said, "I'll do more than that I will ship you the entire program and you can do with it what you want."

Two days later, I had what he had: a plan.

Book 5: Chapter 9: A Secret Plan

After I read through Target 90's, I took it to my campaign chairman Frank Renner.

Frank, an attorney by trade, liked it and suggested that we keep Cisneros' format. We did, in fact, we copied it darn near verbatim.

We called on Wayne Flittner, partner-owner of Ross Advertising, my advertising committee chairman to give us some help.

Frank and Wayne, of course, were not getting paid anything, but helping me out of the kindness of their hearts.

Anyway, the 3 of us promised not to tell anyone about Target 90's.

Gura, afterall, was in with the in-crowd. On his staff were a bunch of hot shots from Caterpillar, plus some state and city officials. And we didn't want anyone getting word of what we were up to. I didn't even tell my wife for fear of our plan getting out.

I don't know that it would have mattered had it gotten out, we were so far behind in the polls and everything. But we kept it all hush-hush.

In our minds, Gura's team had no plan, except to say, "We know how to run a city."

And yet the city was in the worst state possible. Nearly 18% unemployment, high interest rates, over 30,000 people unemployed, it was a disaster.

So if we had any chance at all of beating him in the general election, we had to unveil our plan at a very, very opportune time.

Wayne Flittner took the plan back to his advertising agency and recreated the thing. He did it under very secret conditions, nobody in the place knew except for one other person. He redrew it, put it on a colored board, and changed the name from Target 90's to Forward Peoria!

And now that we had it all together, we waited.

Book 5: Chapter 10: An Easel, huh?

We knew that we had two head-to-head debates coming up against my opponent, Dan Gura. The first one was on a Sunday night, primetime, 7 o'clock, right after 60 minutes on WEEK, channel 25.

Now if you remember, channel 25 and I were good friends because of St. Jude. So, anyway, on the night of the debate, as I walked into the studio I said, "I need an easel."

"What do you need an easel for?"

"Well frankly it's a secret. But I have something that I want to unveil during the debate."

"We can't do that for you, Jim, unless your opponent has an equal opportunity."

"Well, give it to him."

"Give him an easel, huh?"

"Yeah. You can go tell him that I am going to unveil something, a program, during this debate."

Well, after some short discussion back and forth, the Gura clan finally conceded, I could use the easel.

The first of our two remaining debates took place about 9 days before the election.

The debate was held in the WEEK studios. Tom MacIntyre headed up a panel of three to ask the questions.

Naturally, they always start with the ordinary "Who are you?" and "Why are you running?" and all that stuff.

But about 12 minutes into the questioning, someone asked us, "What do you plan to do as mayor, regarding the city's economic development?"

Dan Gura had the first chance to answer the question. And he had no program to speak of, except to say, "I am going to fix this and I'm going to fix that."

In my opinion, it was a lot of political mumbo-jumbo, but no straight-talk or plan of action.

When Dan was done talking, I said, "I'm glad you asked that question. I have a proven program. A program that worked in San Antonio, Texas, and I believe it is a program that will absolutely work in Peoria, Illinois. But I can't do it alone. It's going to take people."

And so now with my television experience, I'm looking right directly into the camera and address those watching at home.

"Those of you who are watching tonight," I said, "I have a message for you: for no one but you.

"This is your community. It's not my opponent's

community. It's not mine. It's your community. If you are satisfied with the conditions of this community, that being the unemployment, the boarded up stores downtown, the ugly-looking riverfront, with the food lines, I've seen the proud families lined up in front of the Salvation Army and South Side mission waiting for food, and if you are satisfied with those conditions, then I will tell you like Ronald Reagan said once, vote for my young opponent."

Earlier in the campaign, Dan had made some wisecrack remarks about me being a senior citizen.

"If you are satisfied," I repeated, "vote for my young opponent. If you are not satisfied as I am. I am not satisfied. Here is an opportunity for you to enjoin yourself, to jump in, and become a part of the new city of Peoria. Something that all of us can be a part of."

And with that, I unveiled the Forward Peoria! plan which was sitting on the easel.

The debate, like most all, was timed. Each candidate had an allotted amount of time with which to answer the questions.

I believe I had only 2 minutes to answer this particular question. And I think I used that up before I even unveiled the plan. But, since no one stopped me, I just kept right on talking.

"Forward Peoria! is a bottom's up, people kind of program, where the people of the community are involved," I explained.

Altogether, there are sixteen committees, Enterprise Zone, Southtown, Neighborhoods & Parks,

Utilities, City Services, Human Services, Small Business, Labor/Management Relations, Venture Capital, Health Care Services, River & Riverfront, Foreign Trade Zone, Transportation, Education & Training, Funds & Scourcing, and Media. Plus we had a Budget committee.

As I pointed to each committee, I would ask the viewers, "Where do you fit? If you feel that your expertise is in any one of these committeees, please, please call the campaign office tomorrow and give us your name and address and we will find the right slot for you and you can become a part of Forward Peoria! And you can help revive our community."

The Second Debate

The first debate was on a Sunday night, and on Tuesday night, one week before the April 2, 1985, Consolidated General Election, we had our second hour long television debate.

This time it was on ABC, channel 19, at 7 o'clock, right after the news hour.

We were fearful that maybe they might come up with some kind of a program to counteract ours. The polls showed that Gura's camp was ahead by some 25 or 30 points.

I can only guess, because they were so far ahead in the polls, that the Gura camp didn't feel the need to change their strategy.

They also had the backing of the labor unions, the state representatives, and the local government, so they were feeling pretty confident in themselves, I would imagine.

There were different people sitting on this debate panel, but they were asking us basically the same questions as before. And as before, I unveiled my easel to show the Forward Peoria! plan.

Gura countered by saying, "I have the expertise. I have 6 years worth of experience on the Peoria City Council."

"If I had 6 years worth of experience on the council and the city was in the condition it is in today," I said, "I'd be ashamed. Absolutely ashamed."

I pulled out all of the stops, it was my last effort.

The Week Before the Election

We were taking phone calls all day long. Wherever I'd go, people would say, "Hey I'd like to serve on (such and such) committee."

The day after the first debate, I started carrying a little notepad and pen around with me. "Great. Give me your name, phone number, and address; we'll get back to you." I wasn't going to let nobody get away.

In the time span of that 9 days, from the time I first unveiled Forward Peoria! up to the night before the General Election, our campaign had collected over 500 names.

Over 500 people had volunteered to serve on different committees. Over 500 people wanted to get involved and make their community a better place to live.

Even if I lose this election, I thought to myself, I'm happy to know that there are people out there who care. I'm happy to know that there are people who want to help, and that there are people who love this community as much as I do.

If you remember, in the February primary, Gura had won 114 out of 120 precincts.

And we were down about 30 points in the polls the week before the General Election.

But after introducing Forward Peoria!, the tables were turned. I think I beat him in 106 or 107 out of 120 precincts, which was a complete turnaround.

And so I was elected Mayor of Peoria, Illinois, on April 2 of 1985.

Forward Peoria!

One of the first things I did, after I got the news, was to call Henry Cisneros down in San Antonio.

I thanked him over and over again.

Target 90's and Forward Peoria! were fundamentally the same plan. But Henry's executive committee was organized slightly different than what we had proposed.

Henry had set it up so that he was the chairman.

I was not the chairman. Because to me, the plan was about involving as many different people as possible. I simply saw it as a people plan, and it belonged to the people.

And there were over 500 people who wanted to get plugged in.

First we needed a leader, the top dog, someone to sit as the chair of the executive committee. I appointed my campaign chairman, Frank Renner to that position. And that was simply because Frank Renner understood the Forward Peoria! plan better than anyone else, so he'd be the best one to implement it.

Next, we needed 4 more people sit on that executive committee with Frank Renner.

Now, those 5 people would oversee the 16 different committees, like Southtown, Riverfront, and so on. And each of those committees would have a chairperson.

So we started screening our pool of 500 volunteers to find the best 16 people to fill those slots. And we didn't want these people to be high profile "big shot" people. We didn't want the state legislators and all the political people. No, we wanted our people to be "the average joe." We wanted our committees chaired by real working people: people who understood the problems and the plight of the families standing in the food line.

Not always, but too many times, the CEO is too busy counting up profits to care about the plight of his workers, and we didn't want those kinds of people either.

We wanted working people that understood what it is like to live paycheck to paycheck; hard working people, who were proud of their community, and willing to serve it.

And those people existed, and we found them.

So, after we found, what we felt, were the best 16 committee chairpersons, we then gave them the responsibility of combing over the names of other people on our list and recruiting the best 20 or 25 to be a part of their team.

So, now, instead of just little old me trying to solve the problems of the community, we had over 300 people working on solving the problems in front of us.

The job of each committee was fundamentally simple. If you were on the Southtown Committee, for example, you're team would come together to discuss the pro's and con's of what action or actions needed to be taken to improve that area of Peoria.

So, a pro could be "the people need to be moved out of their rat infested homes."

The con would be "the city doesn't have the money to buy their homes at this time."

And then the 20 or 25 on that committee would have the responsibility of coming up with a viable, or workable, solution to the problem.

So I really didn't tell them what to do except to say your committee knows the problems, find them, surface them, come back with some solutions and they did.

Forward Peoria! was theirs. They owned it. And because they owned it, it was a huge success.

And Southtown, by the way, was the first problem we solved.

Clergy Coming Together

I don't believe I've told you this part of the story, about my decision to run for Mayor.

One day, shortly after I had announced my intention to run, I received a visit from my next door neighbor, Dr. Ira Galloway.

Dr. Galloway was the pastor at First United Methodist Church. After a long discussion about my intentions, Pastor Galloway openly backed my bid for mayor. He told his congregation several times from the pulpit that he was backing Jim Maloof for mayor of Peoria.

Wow. That was unheard of.

But Pastor Galloway did more for me than just that. He also introduced me to Dr. Bruce Dunn, Senior Pastor at Grace Presbyterian Church.

Now Pastor Dunn and I were two guys who weren't likely to see eye to eye on most issues. But, as the good Lord would have it, at a meeting mediated by Pastor Galloway, Pastor Dunn and myself discussed the tough problems facing our community.

And it wasn't long after that meeting, when Pastor Dunn also openly backed my run for mayor.

And it was then Pastor Dunn who introduced me to Jerry Trecek, the Executive Director of the Peoria Rescue Ministries, and Bishop Ackerman of the St. Paul Episcopalian Church.

Now, certainly, their endorsements meant a lot to me and to my campaign, no question about it.

But the impact of these meetings could really be seen after my election.

I asked each and every one of them, plus many others, if they thought it would be possible to bring together all the Christian leaders of this community, to join together and pray for this community?

After all, Caterpillar and the UAW were still in the middle of a huge contract dispute; the food lines got longer before they got shorter; and people were still leaving this community to look for work in places like Texas and Florida and California.

So with everyone's agreement, we brought together the Christian leaders of the community and unashamedly we began to hold prayer meetings.

We held two interdenominational prayer vigils at the Bradley Field House. About 6 weeks later, we had another one at the Peoria Civic Center.

The first one at Bradley attracted about 4,000 people and the one at the Civic Center attracted about 3,500 people.

And what we did was to involve the Christian leaders in ways they had never been involved before.

Prior to this, the Peoria Christian leadership had never been involved in politics, but because we asked, and because they were willing, we involved them in Forward Peoria!, and they sat on a variety of committees.

My administration got involved with the PCL, the City of Peoria Christian Leadership Council which at that time was a group of about 18 black ministers.

These ministers were eager to participate once they saw the willingness of other ministers to be involved.

On a bi-monthly basis, sometimes every 6 or 7 weeks, I would have an open door meeting, at my office in City Hall, with the leaders of the Black Christian community.

We would talk about ways to open doors for the black community. And we took action by putting them on commissions; involving them with Forward Peoria!; and finding ways to address the issue of the gang violence in Peoria.

We did that successfully for 12 years. I don't know what has happened to it now, but that was absolutely a great relationship.

When people come up to me and say, "What is one of the main things you'd like to be remembered for as the Mayor of Peoria?"

I tell them, "I'd like people to remember that while I was the Mayor of Peoria, Illinois, the Christian community came together and helped rebuild this city."

It was just thrilling to watch them unashamedly step forward.

Where's my Office?

I was a maverick when I went to City Hall in May of 1985.

"It's time we turn this thing back to the people," I'd say.

"Let the people decide. Let the people determine their future." That was my rally cry.

But since I'd spent my entire campaign attacking "the do-nothing city council," and "the do-nothing Chamber of Commerce," I didn't find many friends when I arrived at City Hall.

During that entire month of transition, between the time I had been elected until the time I took office, I had gone down to City Hall everyday.

I found myself stuffed into some ugly old obscure office, no windows, no phone, no nothing. About an 8' x 10' office, that was my pre-mayoral introduction to being the mayor of Peoria.

While 90% of the people down at City Hall didn't like me when I was first elected, there was a woman by the name of Roberta Parks who had my back.

Roberta kind of took me under her wing; she knew city hall backwards and forwards; and she helped me so much, I can't tell you how indebted I am to her.

If it wasn't for the Roberta Park's of this world maybe nothing would get done?

But she wasn't going to let other people's opinion

of me stop her from helping me help our community.

And by working together we did some wonderful things.

And then the second city manager under my tenure was a man by the name of Peter Korn.

Peter was not well-liked in many circles, but he was a no-nonsense kind of guy, a very good businessman.

When we met, on the first day he walked into my office he said, "Mayor?"

I said, "Yep?"

And he said, "I got one job to do, I've got a number of them, but my number one job is to make you look good as mayor. I'll do everything I can to make you look good as mayor. You tell me what you want done and I'll do my best to get it done."

Wow. He was the consummate professional. Who couldn't use a Peter Korn, or two, on their staff.

As mayor, it wasn't just Southtown that I wanted cleaned up, it was the city in general, not just on the South End, but everywhere.

I had noticed in my travels that the cities I remembered, or wanted to return to, were the one's that were attractive and pleasing to the eye.

And Peoria was neither attractive nor pleasing to the eye in 1985. It was a disaster, desperately in need of a make-over.

So another one of the first things I set my sights on was the sorry state of the intersection at Knoxville and War Memorial Drive, where that little triangle is. It was nothing but a weed bed, a real eye sore.

I went to the Peoria Park District and suggested a collaboration between the city and the Park District.

They said, "Yes." And we were off to a good start.

So, once the intersection of Knoxville and War was fixed up, I thought "What could we do to beautify the rest of Knoxville?" You know, from War Memorial Drive south to downtown.

I went to the City Council and suggested that maybe we could line both sides of Knoxville with large flower pots, kind of creating an avenue of flowers.

And they said, "We don't have the money."

And I said, "Well, can't we find the money for a few flower pots?"

So between the Park District, the City Council, and the local businesses, we got it done.

The next thing I know some folks up on the West Bluff came knocking at my door.

They wanted to know if we could help them spiff up their neighborhoods. And as mayor, I had a simple rule, "Whenever possible, do everything you possibly can to help people when they ask for help."

This time, we sat down and wrote letters to our friends and to the business owners in that area, explaining what we wanted to do, and then asked them for a donation to help us. And that was how the Western Avenue Greenway Project got started.

But the momentum didn't stop there. With the support and the positive feedback I started receiving from the community, I knew we could do more. A lot more.

Now, for those of you that are old enough, you'll remember in the 1980's when there used to be billboards and bumper stickers that said, "Would the last one to leave Peoria, Please turn out the lights."

Well, I wanted to counter that. So, I went to the businesses and building owners downtown, and I suggested that they light up their buildings.

I said, "I'd like to see you talk your owners into lighting up these buildings to let people know we're here, and we're not going anywhere. We're here to stay."

The First National Bank building that was the first

one to come on board. And it didn't take very long for the others to follow.

It was so affirming to see that view coming over the Murray Baker Bridge from East Peoria at night, with the Peoria skyline all lit up.

I honestly believe that small gesture of lighting up the skyline became a symbol of hope to our entire community.

And so to me the next logical step was to light up the bridge as well.

Heck, Pittsburgh, San Francisco, all those beautiful cities, all have their bridges lit up. And it looks wonderful.

So I went to the mayor of East Peoria and said, "That river is not there to divide us, why not use it to bring us together? Why don't we cooperate on this?"

And they did cooperate. And we've been finding ways to cooperate with the city of East Peoria ever since.

Just look at the fantastic fireworks these two cities shoot off every Fourth of July. By teaming up and working together the fireworks over the Illinois River went from good to amazing. I think we have one of the best displays of fireworks in the Unites States.

And the whole point being, just like when the people rebuilt the city of Jerusalem, when the people believed and came together, they rebuilt their city.

That's more important to me than anything else, and it can happen, and it can happen right here at home, that's the lesson.

The Singing Mayor

Over the years I've collected a bag full of nicknames. To this day friends and media alike still call me "Mr. Peoria," "Mr. Mayor," and "Your Honor."

But the moniker that I've heard more than any other is "The Singing Mayor."

Honestly, it seems like there's not a day that goes by when someone doesn't refer to me as "The Singing Mayor."

In my first year as the newly elected mayor, we decided to invite some folks from our sister city, Friedrichshafen, Germany, over to visit us here in Peoria, Illinois.

Needless-to-say, they had heard that I was called "the singing mayor," and I didn't want to disappoint, of course, so I started thinking about what I might sing for them?

Over the years, in my repertoire of songs, I used to do a piece called "Wien, Wien, nur du allein." It was an uncomplicated waltz-like tune, with a heartfelt refrain, really it was just a very beautiful love song, and I thought, "Now, this will impress them."

We held a formal gathering at the civic center. I'd say there were about 80 friends from Friedrichshafen on hand, plus about 400 people from the community that also came down to welcome and meet these folks.

I had gone to great lengths to learn enough of the German language to give my opening remarks in their mother tongue. So, for about 3 or 4 minutes I spoke to them in German, given them warm regards and friendly greetings. I even tossed in a few jokes, which they laughed at, so I can only assume they understood me.

And then I concluded by singing *Wien, Wien, nur du allein.*

As a singer, you know if you're on top of your game or not. And wow, this was a good day for me, I could really feel it. The music was just pouring out of me.

But when I looked around and saw the reaction on the people's faces, I thought, "Uh-oh, something is kind of goofy here."

I didn't know what it was, so I just kept singing the song.

And afterwards, right afterwards, my German translator, said, "Do you know what you just did?"

And I said, "No, what did I do?"

And he says, "Well you said that you were singing a German song and how much you loved it and all that stuff, guess what?"

I said, "What?"

And he said, "*Wien, Wien, nur du allein* is not a German song, it's a Viennese song, it's an Austrian song. And that doesn't really set too well with the German people."

Well, egg on my face and all that stuff, I got right back up and I apologized.

And guess what?

They made me sing it again. They even sang the refrain with me.

And of course Germans love to sing and I had a repertoire of German songs, *Du, du, Liegst Mir Im Herzen, Keinen Tropfen Im Becher Mehr*, and a bunch of them.

But the graciousness of those people at that moment, I will forever remember.

Singing Mayor Goes Overseas

Another great thrill for me occurred some years later when a Peoria contention went to visit Friedrichshafen.

Through the efforts of many, we raised enough money to send the Peoria Symphony Orchestra along.

Well, the symphony was doing a concert one evening in their big hall called the Friedrichshafen Grafzeppelinhaus, a place very much like the civic center here in Peoria.

There were roughly 800 local Germans people who had turned out to see this performance.

And somewhere in the middle of it, Bill Wilsen, the conductor of the Peoria Symphony Orchestra, said to the audience, "And now we have a very special surprise for you."

And he introduced the "der singen Burgomeister," or in English "the singing mayor."

I did a medley of songs and did them in German, not Austrian.

And the people there just about went crazy. We received a standing ovation, which is something that rarely happens in Germany.

I mean, it was something extra special, that night was.

I've been blessed with many other wonderful

experiences as the singing mayor. I had the opportunity to sing internationally in France, Germany, China, Korea, and Japan as the Mayor of Peoria, Illinois. Not as Jim Maloof, but as "the Singing Mayor from Peoria, Illinois."

How often does that happen in a lifetime?

I was also fortunate enough to sing with the Old Ladies Choir in Germany and with school children in China.

And no matter where I would be, I would make it a point to learn enough of the native language so that I could always give my opening remarks to the people in their mother tongue, again, be it French, German, Chinese, Korean or Japanese.

And that little effort on my part was always received like a basket of goodwill. And it would always open the door to friendship.

No matter where you are in this world or what you're doing, you should always try to meet people half way. And if that's your minimum effort, I guarantee you'll make a friend.

For all the good that I've done, or tried to do, throughout my life, it still amazes me when I hear "that people don't like Jim Maloof because he was against the riverboat."

I don't apologize for that.

Earlier, I told you about my days in the Army Air Corps; about how Peoria was the laughing stock of the country. It didn't matter if you were fighting Japan in the East, or fighting the Germans in the West, or stationed right here in the states, like I was. Every soldier that left Peoria in the 1940's, came back to Peoria with a desire to clean up our town – to give Peoria a respectable reputation.

Like I said, all the jokes were about Peoria's corrupt politics, gambling, and prostitution. "Live and let live," was the slogan, but it cost our people dearly.

Just think about the way people mock the state of Illinois today. How many Illinois Governors have been accused of wrong doing or are sitting in prison? How many people across the nation, today, are making jokes about Illinois' most recent "former Governor"?

That's the way people talked about Peoria back then. And for many of us, this wasn't acceptable.

So, when the war ended, back in '45, a bunch of us got together and said, "We've got to do something about this."

Finally, by 1952, a bunch of us organized the "Peorians for City Manager." And in 1953, my friend Bob Morgan was elected Mayor of Peoria. For the first time, the Council-Manager form of government was instituted, and the cleaning up of Peoria began.

In 1954, Peoria was voted an "All-American City."

Those efforts were further enhanced when in 1965, a former classmate of mine, Bob Lehnhausen was elected Mayor.

Together, we all worked hard to change the reputation of this town.

And so with all of that said: No, I didn't support the idea of having legalized gambling in Peoria.

But in the end, it didn't really matter what I thought.

There were two applications for the Peoria Gaming License: Jim Jumer, the owner of Jumer's Castle Lodge here in Peoria, and what was commonly referred to as the East Peoria group.

Well, the gaming commission was going to issue thirteen licenses throughout the state of Illinois. That was it, 13.

When the commission was awarding these gaming licenses, Jumer had applied for two, one in the Quad-Cities and one here.

The Commission told him he was going to receive a gaming license, but that each applicant (person or group) could only have 1,200 gaming positions or job openings regardless if he had one or two vessels. It would be Jim

Jumer's choice to pick one or the other or both. He picked the Quad-Cities.

So, that left only the East Peoria group for the available license here Central Illinois.

It is true that Ray Becker did turn in an application for the license, but only after he had heard the news about the Jumer opting for the Quad-Cities. With no applicant from the Peoria side of the river, Ray threw his hat in the ring, so Peoria would have a chance to get the riverboat.

However, Ray's application was turned down because he had missed the application deadline. And that was something the commission decided to stand firm on.

So, by default, you could say, the East Peoria group was awarded the gaming license. In other words, I couldn't have brought the boat here if I wanted to. To use a casino term, the cards had been played for me.

And I still take a lot of blame for the boat not being in Peoria. And if that's the way people think, then so be it, there's not much I can do about it.

I would like to point out that there should at least be a little credit given for what my administration was able to accomplish, in regards to the riverboat.

We did make an agreement with the city of East Peoria, which allowed the riverboat to be temporarily docked on this side of the river until East Peoria was able to make an appropriate permanent home for the boat.

And for a number of years, Peoria received half of the tax revenue which the riverboat casino produced.

Something else few people seems to be aware of, is that Peoria City Manager Peter Korn had struck a deal with the city of East Peoria, way back when, and we (the city of Peoria) are still getting over $4 million dollars a year out of that riverboat deal.

And you know, that's better than nothing, when you consider we didn't have a much of a shot at it in the first place.

I'm still against gambling, on moral grounds, on principle. But, I'll concede that the boat hasn't brought crime or political corruption with it.

But whatever you think in the end, I cannot change that, but I stood up for what I believed was best for this community.

And without hestitation, I'd do it again if I thought it was right.

For all the ups and downs during my 12-year reign as mayor, certainly, there was none so incredibly hurtful as the lawsuit that I was enjoined in 1996.

The women at City Hall were very unhappy with the city manager at that time, and they told me that they were going to do something about it.

It was not Peter Korn, by the way, it was another guy.

And anyway, these women said that they were going to sue the city and so forth.

I had a number of meetings with this city manager and tried to caution him. I suggested that he take the matter seriously. I suggested that he open his door and listen to these women.

Well, he didn't.

And over the course of time, finally, they sued the city of Peoria.

And my secretary at that time, the Mayor's secretary, put herself into that suit and accused me of hugging and, what's the word, sexual harassment.

And that crushed me.

All along the way, I thought I was helping her, encouraging her, helping to make a better life for herself.

I had brought her out of an $18,000 dollars a year job; made her my secretary; and at the time of the lawsuit she was making about $70,000 dollars a year.

But to be accused falsely, it was just one of the worst times of my entire life. And I was 75-years old at the time for goodness sake. But let me just tell you, unless you've been through something like that, you don't really know what it's like.

As soon as the accusation hits the news, the general public makes the assumption that it must be true after all, "We read it in the paper."

And the media makes it sound as outlandish and over-the-top as possible. You stop being a person, and become a vehicle for the press to sell their product. So, yeah, that was hurtful too.

When the news broke an attorney by the name of Roy Davis called.

"Do you have a lawyer?"

"No."

"Well, you are going to need one, and I'm your guy. You will not have a single cent of cost. You've helped our city and now it's our turn to help you."

Roy became, and still is, a great friend.

God bless and Thanks Roy.

Another positive, when trouble like that pops up, you quickly learn who your real friends are.

You get to witness, not necessarily by words, but by actions, the people who support you. You have a clearer understanding of which people liked you because you were on top, and which one's liked you because you are you.

And I've discovered that I've been very blessed. And I thank the good Lord every day; I have a lot of very good friends and the best family in the world.

And one last note on this topic. Shortly after my name was tossed into that lawsuit, a group of women outside of City Hall, you know, just women within the community, started wearing these T-shirts that read, *I hugged the mayor and loved it.*

So, there was a little something to smile about through that entire fiasco as well.

What We Accomplished

When I took over as mayor in 1985, Peoria's economy had literally hit bottom. Caterpillar the community's largest employer was losing money at the rate of $1 billion dollars a year.

Thousands were either laid off or given early retirements; unemployment neared 20%; and what was once a thriving downtown, now saw stores closed and boarded up.

And in my line of business, over 5,000 homes were listed for sale – many of them having been foreclosed.

This is what I inherited.

Of course, we put together Forward Peoria! and found ways to get the citizenry involved. Plus, we got the clergy involved with the city in ways it had never been involved before.

We worked on beautifying the city. And by 1989 Peoria was once again named an All-American City. And I was re-elected for a second term.

My administration continued to diligently work on getting the community back on solid economic footing.

We oversaw the redevelopment and rebuilding of the downtown with major initiatives in city government which included the Twin Towers and the Becker Building.

In my third administration, we turned that solid

economic footing into years of prosperity in the 1990's.

And we worked hard to attract new businesses as well as promoting the retention and expansion of existing businesses.

One of the major highlights of the third term was the introduction of 3 growth cells on the north side of our city.

When I say "north side growth cells" I'm talking about

1) Out on north Knoxville, in the area of Northminster Presbyterian Church, out that way.

2) The new Allen Road, out where Wal-Mart, Menard's, and all of those new businesses are located.

3) Out Route 150, out where the Shoppes at Grand Praire and all of that new development is happening.

What once were cornfields are now happy little subdivisions and busy little shopping malls, which provide a large stream of tax revenue for the city.

Our administration put in place the water and sewer incentives to encourage these growth cells. I mean, these thing don't happen on their own.

And we have seen the expansion of Pioneer Industrial Parkway as another result of these cells.

And the most important part of developing those growth cells is that it got our City Council, the Peoria County Board, Township officials, unions, and businesses all working together like one big family.

What a great feeling, helping it become a reality.

Golden Era of Harmony

Illinois, as I've mentioned, has had a long and storied past with political corruption. Illinois is sometimes referred to as "the wild west of politics."

In fact, more recently FBI special agent Robert Grant announced, upon the arrest of Illinois Governor Rod Blagojevich, "If it is not the most corrupt state in the United States, it's certainly one hell of a competitor."

With all the drama the political scene in Illinois creates, or has created, it's easy to forget that there once was a golden era of getting along here in Illinois, from 1986 to 1997.

And some of the key players in Central Illinois during that era included Jim Edgar; Bob Michel; Ray LaHood; Mike McCoy; Chuck Schofield; Dave Koehler; George Shadid; Kevin Lyons; Don Fites; and some great council members, along with Jim Maloof.

We were sort of the political and community leaders of that era and we got along just famously. We got along so well with each other because we all had only one thing in mind and that was to make this community a better place to live.

If more people focus on their community and not themselves, if more people would turn to roles of servant leadership, then more positive and empowering things could be happening right now, right here at home.

And if you're a young person who wants to get involved, I encourage you and challenge you to look at the life of Christ as your model for leadership.

Christ was a people person, he was all about people, teaching people, leading people, and serving people.

And if you want to be a great leader in this world, or just within your own community, then learn to put people first. Because people matter, in fact, they are all that matter.

And I believe in our golden era of harmony, that's what each and every single one of us tried to do, to put people first.

And if we could do it, so can you.

BOOK 6

The Memoirs of Jim Maloof

After three terms as mayor of Peoria, I did not seek re-election. I had served for 12 years, 3 terms, and was almost 80-years old.

I probably would have thrown my hat in the ring one more time, but it was Trudy that didn't want me to run again. And like always, if she said so, then it was so.

When word reached Illinois Governor Jim Edgar that I wouldn't be running for a forth term, he immediately nominated me for a position on the state's Human Rights Commission.

The Illinois Human Rights Commission is set up to hear cases of discrimination based on sex, age, race, color, criminal past, handicap, and the like. Mostly we would hear allegations of discrimination from the work place.

And then Governor George Ryan reappointed me to that post when he took over the reigns.

But that too has run its course.

Sometimes, I think I miss being mayor, but it takes time. I guess what I really miss the most is the talking over ideas, giving people the ball and watching them dive into a project.

In 2000, St. Jude Children's Hospital Midwest
Affiliate Clinic moved across the road and into the
Children's Hospital of Illinois, located inside of St.
Francis Hospital.

The decision to move wasn't an easy one, as
Methodist had done so much for St. Jude and children of
St. Jude.

It was upon the advice of John McCallister, a
doctor of pediatric oncology and hematology, who
recognized that St. Francis now possessed most, if not
all, the sub-specialty doctors that St. Jude needed so
badly.

St. Francis had these sub-specialty doctors
because of the Children's Hospital of Illinois.

And so together, and rather privately, Memphis
and St. Francis orchestrated the move.

We feel truly blessed that St. Francis was willing
to make this kind of commitment to our kids and for our
kids, our precious, precious kids.

Again, I can't overstate what Methodist Hospital
had done for us for 27 years: the 27 years that we were
there at Methodist, they gave us whatever we needed,
anything and everything, they just took care of it, and
we will always be indebted to Methodist for what they've
done for St. Jude.

Richard Unes is another Lebanese-Peorian who has dedicated his life to St. Jude. And I just can't write a book about my life, and my involvement with St. Jude, without mentioning my friend Richard Unes.

If you recall, Richard and I worked together on the first Teen March. He's been involved with St. Jude darn near as long as I have.

He used to drive me to speaking engagements way back in '60's. And of course, everything we've ever done for St. Jude has been as volunteers. So all the cost of all the traveling we've done has come straight out of our own pockets. But it never bothered Richard, he was all too happy to help.

And when I say all expenses, I mean the hotels, the dinners, the gas, everything came out of our own pockets – and it's still that way with St. Jude today. All the Board Members are volunteers and responsible for all of their own expenses.

Another guy that helped us out a lot in those early days too was Sam George. Sam was in the punch board business, which I wasn't fond of, but he was always willing to fork over the dough to pay for the dinners we held and stuff like that. We couldn't have made it without him either.

Same could be said of Dan Deeb, we couldn't have made it in those early years without his involvement.

But anyway, back to Richard Unes: in 1996, I nominated Richard for a seat on the Board of Directors for St. Jude Children's Research Hospital in Memphis.

He became the chairman of the new building committee for St. Jude. Richard worked for a very prominent building contractor here in Peoria. He's a very gifted and talented project engineer. And so with his vision and experience as a builder, just about every single new St. Jude building that you now see in Memphis has Richard's fingerprint on it.

I believe they've done something like $1 billion dollars worth of construction down there during the sixteen years he been on the new building committee.

He's really a remarkable man. And he's done a remarkable job. This year Richard is serving as Second Vice President on the ALSAC National Board of Directors, and in 2011 he will serve as the National Executive Director of ALSAC.

So, that's quite an accomplishment. And I am very proud of him.

Hardly anyone is more dedicated or has a stronger passion for St. Jude than my friend, and Peoria County Sheriff, Mike McCoy.

Michael has come along since organizing that first St. Jude run held over at Landmark, when they raised "a couple of hundred dollars."

To his credit, he is past-President of the St. Jude Midwest Affiliate Clinic Board of Directors.

And he has taken over the reigns for me as the new

host of the annual St. Jude telethon here in Peoria.

The St. Jude Memphis to Peoria Run has raised over $2 million dollars in each of the past three years, which brings the total raised by this run to over $20 million dollars, making it one of the largest fundraising events in the nation for St. Jude.

My good friend Mike McCoy, to this day, still runs in the event he founded. And I am very proud of all he has done. And I have confidence in all that he will continue to do for St. Jude.

In 2000, Rose Marie Thomas, Danny's wife passed away. She was buried on the grounds of St. Jude Children's Research Hospital.

And on March 29, 2001, my wife, Trudy, passed away. We were married just 3 months short of 60 years.

She was a quiet one in the marriage and obviously, I was the loud one, but more than that, she was a guiding force in my life. I was faithful to her throughout our 60 years, and she was very, very loyal to me, I know.

I believe she was sent to me by the Lord. And like the song I used to sing, she was the wind beneath my wings.

I can not say enough about her. With all of my activities, the singing, the sports, the community events, and St. Jude, through it all, she never ever complained. She never tried to stop me from participating in the activities I was involved in.

It was quite the opposite, in fact, she'd say, "The Lord has plans for you, go ahead and do it."

That was her story, "The Lord has plans for you, do it."

She was a great encourager. She'd pick me up when I was down. She'd brush me off and send me back out to face my critics, and I knew she'd always be right beside me.

What people didn't know about her is that she loved being called upon by the Guardian Angel Home out on Heading Avenue. It was her community service.

About twice a week they would call her to come out and pick up one of the youngsters at the Home and take him to the dentist or some other kind of doctor's visit.

And she would do that, but nobody in this town really knew about it. She preferred it that way. But that was one of her ways of giving back, just being able to do something in her own way, and without a lot of fanfare.

She was a great, great lady; a fantastic mom, and just an all-around beautiful person.

And there isn't a day that goes by that I don't miss her. And on that day when the good Lord finally does call me home, I'll be running to her.

Now remember, a while back, I had made mention that the NBA had introduced two new teams into their league, the Toronto Raptures and the Vancouver Grizzles.

Well, 2001, the Grizzlies moved to Tennessee and became the Memphis Grizzlies.

In 2002, legendary Bradley Braves basketball coach Dick Versace became the General Manager of that Memphis team.

Sidney Lowe was the coach, and on his staff there were a few other Peorians, one was Tom Penn, Jr., another was Dana Davis, who was an outstanding volunteer while here in Peoria.

So that summer, Sheriff McCoy and his Memphis to Peoria Run committee, including myself, were in Memphis on some St. Jude business.

We decided to take advantage of our connections with the Grizzlies staff and stopped over to the Forum there on Beale Street to shoot the breeze.

We mentioned our visit to Dick Shadyac, who was now the National Executive Director of ALSAC.

Dick then called up Mike Heisley, the majority owner of the Grizzlies, and invited him, and a few other people within the organization over to visit the hospital.

And they fell in love with St. Jude and agreed to do something to support the kids.

And they did, they built the Memphis Grizzlies House, or Grizzly house as we call it. It's similar to the Ronald McDonald House. It now serves as the primary short-term stay facility in Memphis.

It's a state-of-the-art facility that can house up to 100 families per night.

They are kind of like furnished hotel rooms or apartments where the family can stay together while the patient is being treated. There's a big dining room, a fitness room, laundry facilities, and even a playground.

Oh, it's something to see. All of their groceries are provided. They need to ask for nothing, which is how St. Jude has always operated.

Anyway, the Grizzlies donated $5 million dollars in the beginning, and have donated several millions more for updates and expansion.

At 87 years of age, I was still driving myself to and from work.

A year before Trudy died, we had down sized our home, and we had moved closer to the office.

On Wednesday, November 16, I was rather seriously hurt in a car wreck.

I broke my neck.

The doctors said that at my age, it can't be fixed, so I've just had to live with it.

I still have a full-time job and all these activities, and I'm still a man on the go.

It's always been that way, A broken neck won't keep me at home.

And I'm loving every minute of it.

Book 6: Chapter 7: Supporting the Arts

In 2001, I received the first ever ArtsPartner of the Year Award for my role in supporting the arts in Central Illinois. It was a tremendous honor because the winner of that award is nominated and then selected by the members of the local arts community. And I guess, they wanted someone who had been involved over a long period or duration of time.

And, of course, I have been around now a long, long time. So, I qualified there anyway.

As I said earlier, my love of music came from my mother. But, over the years, I've come to embrace all forms of art. And I've always tried to encourage the community to support the local Arts and Entertainment.

In fact, when I was the mayor, wherever I went around the country, I would tell the people how proud we are to have an appreciation of the arts in here Peoria.

And I have always believed that people are more likely to move to your community if they know you have a living, breathing, growing, and supported arts community.

So, again, I would tell people, wherever I went, "Hey, Peoria has got a great Symphony" or Opera or Ballet, or whatever.

I actually got involved with the Peoria Ballet over 40 years ago, when Shirley Pizer, one of the group's founders, asked me to sing *The Star-Spangled Banner* at their first show. And that was back in 1966, I think, at the Shrine Mosque Temple.

And then in the early 1990's, I became more actively involved after watching the all-volunteer staff struggle to keep the organization running.

One day, I had been down at the Peoria Civic Center and had seen this wonderful ballet performed.

And afterwards, I stopped in over at the Peoria Ballet offices, then located over on Hamilton, and I saw half a dozen parents, moms and dads, and grandparents; one was on her hands and knees cleaning the bathroom; one was dusting the office; and the another was answering the phone. All being led by Suzie Bearce-Pschirrer, the business director of the Peoria Ballet.

Anyway, I couldn't help but notice how passionate they were about making sure that the ballet stayed alive, so their kids could learn the art of dance.

"Wow," I thought, "Somebody's got to do something to help these people out."

And I did.

I got on the phone and called a bunch of people. And with the help of Caterpillar and Henry Hollings, we organized a meeting. And within, I'd say, two weeks time, we had a new Board of Directors and a whole new direction.

And they managed to save it. Sort-of like what we did with Forward Peoria! We got the right people involved higher up and let them guide the people with the passion.

And I thought it was vital to do this, because, I believe that people want to live in a community where there are things to do, and activities that their children can take part in. That's the way I see it; and that is the importance of it: The arts matter.

And as sort of a thank you for what I did back then, on my 90th birthday, which was on October 18, 2009, the Peoria Ballet put on a special performance for me –and the community- at the Scottish Rite Cathedral.

Book 6: Chapter 8: 90th Birthday Celebration

On my birthday, the family had a little party for me at Agatucci's Restaurant over on North University. There was plenty of pizza, soda, beer, and cake to go around for all.

They invited about 100 and some people, friends both old and new. Marshall Lipkin gave an inspiring speech and then my son's Michael and Nick both told little anecdotes.

And then Kevin Lyons got up and did some jokes and whatnot, as he does every year. It was such a good time. And, so, that was my private, family and friends, birthday party.

And then on Monday night, Eric Yetter and the Peoria Ballet held a special performance in my honor. It was open to the public and everyone and anyone who wanted to come was invited.

There were probably over 300 people that came to the show. And there were probably twenty kids that participated in the performance. They were really terrific. I mean, you just have to appreciate what those young people do. They work so hard learning discipline; learning dance; and learning to be better community-minded people. I just think it's one of the better things around. So I support it and work for it. And they did a marvelous job.

One of my favorite songs of all-time is Louis Armstrong's *What a Wonderful World*. Well, lo and behold, one of the dancers, Lauren Trerice, she performed an original piece to that music, God Bless her. I used to sing that song to Trudy all the time. So that was very special.

But the whole thing was fantastic. I was really moved by it all.

And we managed to raise $30,000 dollars for the Peoria Ballet that night. And that was the best birthday present anyone could have given me.

We took a small part of the proceeds from that night to start the James A. Maloof Ballet Endowment Fund. Thanks to Mrs. Dave Ransburg (Zan).

Afterwards, downstairs in the basement of the Cathedral, they held a little shin-dig in my honor. State's Attorney Kevin Lyons played emcee for the evening. And he can be so darn funny, he had them all laughing.

Congressmen Aaron Shock and David Leitch were on hand to give some remarks about the old man.

I sang *My Way*.

And then I reminded everyone there, I said, "If anything should come out of tonight, I would hope that whatever little bit I've offered in stimulating enthusiasm for this great community is an example of what all of you can do,"

And for all the love and all the support in that room that night, it was very humbling.

So, now, here officially began, the 10-year countdown to my 100th birthday party.

The Old Guy of Politics

It's kind of nice, when you're in your nineties, to still be asked for your opinion. I guess I'm something like the old guy of politics around here.

People call me up all of the time asking me about this or that.

I field questions from U.S. Representatives, from current councilmen, and many others.

Recently, Phil Luciano of the *Peoria Journal Star* rounded up some of us senior citizens for a series of roundtable debates.

The discussions, led by Luciano, are between Senator George Shadid, Pete Vonachen, and myself.

We sit around and hash over questions like the positives and negatives of the proposed "Build A Block museum," which hasn't gone anywhere in a dozen years.

I'm for the Riverfront Museum, of course.

I spent a lot of my time and energy, when I was mayor, trying to revive the downtown area, to bring life back to the riverfront, which was nearly abandoned at one time. My friend Jim Baldwin deserved much of the credit.

Anyway, the panel gets to toss around ideas on the best way to fix the school district. We discuss how the state budget affects the city, all those kinds of things.

And I guess in the end, I feel honored that people still care what I think. I feel honored to know that there are people who acknowledge and are respectful of my lifetime of hard work.

And as I've said, I still keep a very high profile in this community, probably higher now then when I was mayor.

And the best part is nobody can get mad at me now because I can't cast any votes.

People just come to me for advice.

I'd like to believe I've done some good along the way. And I hope I can continue to contribute tomorrow and the days after that.

On July 16, 2010, the OSF Saint Francis Medical Center unveiled its new $280 million dollar Milestone Project, the largest privately funded project in Peoria's history.

The expansion houses the OSF Children's Hospital of Illinois. And inside of that is our newly expanded St. Jude Midwest Affiliate.

Richard Unes helped convince the St. Jude board to allocate the money, the $11 million dollars, and resources necessary to make this happen.

So, by partnering with St. Francis and the Children's Hospital, we can provide more space and a better facility to treat sick kids.

The entire new addition is bright and colorful, to make the children feel more at ease. The floors are themed. The art work and even the furniture are designed to be pleasing to the eyes of a child. And the technology is top of the line. It's truly fantastic.

When the Affiliate first opened, we had nineteen patients and since then we have treated over 1,000 patients here in Peoria.

Also in the beginning, all newly diagnosed patients continued to be referred to Memphis for initial treatment; and they received their follow-on treatments here in Peoria -- only having to travel to Memphis once a year.

Now, in the last 10 years or so, some childhood

cancers are treated completely at the Midwest Affiliate, without the need for even the initial treatment in Memphis.

And I feel like the good Lord has blessed this community again. And it's an honor to live here.

About a year before the new hospital was scheduled to open, I received a call from our St. Jude Midwest Affiliate Chairman Mike McCoy and he said, "Jim, we want to name the clinic after you: The Jim Maloof Midwest Affiliate clinic."

And I said, "You will not."

And he said, "Uh-oh," thinking that he was in big trouble.

"Well," he said, "What do you think we should name it?"

And I said, "How about the Jim and Trudy Maloof Midwest Affiliate clinic."

I'm sure that I can speak for Trudy as well on this matter. We are honored and humbled that they would want to put the Maloof name on the Affiliate.

And this honor is like the crowning jewel in a lifetime of achievements, accomplishments, and hard work.

I can only hope that my vision, my dedication, my drive, and my leadership have contributed to the success of ALSAC, to the success of St. Jude, and to the success of the Midwest Affiliate.

And having said that, I'd like to reiterate what I've

always preached, what I've always insisted, it's not about me. It's not about us.

This brand new facility is for the children.

This brand new facility is about helping the children.

And it's about seeing to it that every cancer stricken child has access to the best medical treatment we can possible provide for them.

And knowing that every day we work hard, we are one day closer to a cure for all children.

Today the survival rate is over 90%, in most types of childhood cancer. And it would be easy to rest now, to slow down and say, "Whew, we've almost made it."

But we can't do that. We can't relax, we can't slow down, we can't afford to look in the eyes of that 10% and give a half-hearted "we tried."

That's not acceptable. That's not good enough. It's just not good enough. It will never be good enough until every child has the same opportunity, an opportunity to live.

To live a healthy life, to grow up and become a productive member of our society, of our community, that's our goal for every child.

And for those children we will keep working. And knowing that we are doing everything that can be done, that makes me very, very, happy.

I still go to my realty office over on West Pioneer Parkway every work day, five days a week. I can't retire. I don't know what I'd do with myself. I think I'd be lost. All I know how to do is work: work hard.

I am doing less though. In 2001, shortly after Trudy died, I handed the keys over to my son Michael. Michael's now the president of Jim Maloof Realtor. He takes care of the day-to-day operations.

I'm on hand to answer questions, give advice, and call on our customers. I do a bit of anything and everything. I make sure everyone is satisfied, and that everyone is doing their job.

By the time I handed the business over to my son, it had grown into one of the foremost residential real estate firms in the Peoria area. Thanks to a great staff and great sales personnel.

In sales alone, the business had grown in excess of $400 million dollars with fifteen offices throughout Central Illinois.

It astounds me when I look back on how far the business has come since 1969. Starting a realty company on a $3,000 dollar loan, you couldn't hardly do that today.

This recent recession hurt us too, like everybody else.

But Michael's done a fine job with the company, and under his guidance, sales are up in Central Illinois compared to the past two years (2008-2009). So, that is good news.

Michael took some risks during the recession. He decided to keep all of our branches open and maintain our sales staff of over 200 agents. Sales fell for two years running, but we stayed where we were. And things have improved.

My son called it "an act of faith."

He's a chip off the ol' block.

And I'm so very happy that my son has taken the reigns of the old man's business, just like I took over the reigns of my dad's business.

Book 6: Chapter 12: Nick and Janice

While Michael inherited my business sense, my son Nick inherited my musical gifts.

He can sing and play piano with the best of them. He also inherited my extrovert personality. Nick is always having a good time, enjoying life, and laughing.

He even moved out West for a while to pursue a career as a professional musician.

While it didn't turn out the way he had hoped, I'm proud of him for giving it a try.

I thank the good Lord that he's back home, to entertain the family during our gatherings, to sing a song and tell a story or two.

After witnessing a gentleman donating $1 million dollars to St. Jude, Nick was so inspired that he wrote a catchy little song called *Having Heritage*. He's always coming up with some new tune.

He owns his own company. He's married to Olga, and they have three beautiful children, Nick, Michy, and Markie.

Unlike the boys, my daughter Janice takes after Trudy.

She was in Chicago for 12 years, during the 80's and 90's, and she had a German Shepherd police dog, Baron. She trained that dog to go into nursing homes, and senior citizen facilities, where the patients just love animals. An animal can be the best medicine some of those folks can have. She used to do that 2-3 nights a week.

There's a lot of her grandma in her too. She is an unbelievable young lady.

And since I broke my neck, she's my caregiver. She takes care of me. In fact, she gave up her job at Riverside Community Church, just so she could be free to look after me.

I can't drive anymore, so she shuttles me to and from work, plus all the other places and events I have to go to.

There's no slowing me down, but I couldn't do it without my daughter.

She adjusts her social calendar for me. Heck, she hardly has a social life now because of me. But like she did with her mother, in the last years of Trudy's life, when her health was failing, Janice took care of her, and now she's taking care of me.

My life would not be the same without her. Like her mom, she is truly the wind beneath my wings.

And I also want to mention our companion Maxy. He's the best friend a man could have. He's a six-year old Chihuahua. And he never misses anything. Frequently, Maxy can be found at the office, the staff calls him "Office Max." He goes to the St. Jude Telethon, and was at the building dedication.

He's a big part of our family. And I love him darn near like a child.

What was once about an acre of land has now grown into prominence in the medical world. St. Jude, in Memphis, is now nearly 100 acres, and they keep growing and growing and growing.

Never did Danny Thomas dream that he would one day be the founder of the number one organization of its kind in the world.

When he asked us to raise $300,000 dollars a year to keep the doors of St. Jude open, it didn't seem like that much.

Today, the budget for St. Jude in Memphis, plus the 5 affiliates across the country, is over $1.5 million a day.

Let me say that again, today, the day-to-day operating cost of St. Jude is over $1.5 million dollars per day.

If we had known that back in 1957, I'm not sure we would have done it.

Actually, that's not true at all, because when we look back at all the lives that have been saved, we'd do it all over again in a New York minute.

And I still remember, just like it was yesterday, when Danny was telling us his story. We were so moved by what he said. He just made believers out of all of us, certainly out of me. And as of that moment, I more or less dedicated my entire life to helping him in this cause.

I wouldn't have wanted to miss a moment of it. Especially, those unforgettable minor miracles, like when Danny met Billy Johnson. And Billy giving him 75 cents to help the sick children.

I mean, wow. Nobody saw that coming. There's not a doubt in my mind, God had his hand in that one.

Danny would then take that little white envelope all around the world and raise millions and millions of dollars with that story.

As the hospital has kept growing, the St. Jude statue in Memphis has been moved on 3 different occasions, but Billy Johnson's 75 cents is still in that cornerstone, visible and for all to see. And the envelope is there in the hallway, along with the story for all to read.

When I look back on my life, it's as organized and wonderful as any well written script, full of surprises and unbelievable blessings.

I had never heard of ESA when Marilyn Knuth first called me. In over 40 years of service, ESA has now raised over $160 million dollars for St. Jude. That is amazing, absolutely amazing.

I am even a sister member of ESA. I got my sisterhood honor before Danny got his and I used to kid the daylights out of him about that.

But anyway, the more and more I think about all that has happened the more and more convinced I am that the good Lord has had his hand in the whole thing.

The Memphis to Peoria Run is another example.

That just blows my mind when I look at what has been accomplished. The first run raised $22,000 dollars. The Memphis to Peoria Run now involves 19 cities and over 1,600 runners. And since 1982, the Run has raised over $20 million dollars for St. Jude.

Wow.

And it just continues to gain momentum.

And the Peoria Affiliate and telethon have now gone over the $5 million dollar mark per year, in fundraising.

And it's not just individual people and civic organizations pitching it, it's also companies from the community.

And I am so grateful for companies like Bergner's and WEEK-TV, companies that have made a conscientious decision to participate. They didn't have to, but they chose to.

I know, at one time, it was costing WEEK in excess of $50,000 a year to put the St. Jude telethon on the air. That includes loss of advertising dollars, lost news time, the cost of production people, and equipment and all of that stuff. For over 30 years, their investment in St. Jude has been well over $1 million dollars, perhaps closer to $2 million dollars.

And likewise with Bergner's, they have continued to be our faithful sponsor. In fact, I believe they have supported St. Jude longer than any other company in the entire nation. And their employees raise somewhere between $40,000 and $50,000 dollars every year for St. Jude. Certainly, their investment is well over $1 million dollars as well.

As individuals volunteer, and as organizations get involved, and companies place their support behind this great cause, great things continue to happen.

And if you don't believe me, ask the parents. Ask the parents of the youngsters whose lives are being saved.

It's just unreal.

Every time I reflect back over the events of my life, I can't help but see them all tied together. These stories, collectively and individually, make me believe that much more in what is happening and every time one of those happenings occur, it just strengthened my conviction that God has had his hand in this whole thing.

I believe that God has had his hand on my entire life. That he has asked me to take on the role of helping people, especially the children.

I believe that God had a design for my entire life, if I knew it or not, if I understood it or not.

And I feel that in my particular case, my talents were used to love God and love your neighbor, a very strong biblical phrase: love God and love your neighbor in a manner that will be pleasing to Him.

The bottom line is this: our lives are enriched with the satisfaction of knowing that we did something good along the way.

God had a role for me, and no doubt, and that is why I continue to believe more and more in the miracles that he continues to sow upon us as individuals.

Each day my prayers are not for me, but for the ability to help people; for the ability to help our community; and for the ability to help those who are in need and suffering.

And so those are my prayers everyday. Not for me, but for others. And I pray that way each and every day, morning and night, just knowing in my heart and in my soul that God is listening.

And when you finally put this book down, and

ponder on it a while, let it perkilate in the back of your mind for some time, and sooner or later you will come to understand, or come to see, that when I tell you about these minor things, minor miracles happening, they happen within each one of us.

They happen because of you and because of me.

They happen in spite of you and in spite of me.

But the more you connect the events, the more you believe that there is something about this whole thing that brings us all together.

Yes, I believe God has a plan for everyone's life.

And yes, I believe that our lives are all connected, they all intertwine.

And I believe that God wants us to make a difference in the lives of other people.

And that's why you can't spend your life sitting on your duff watching tv, or glued to the computer, or just whittling it away, because someone out there needs you. Someone out there, that maybe you've never met, or you'll never meet, needs you to get involved and make a difference, because maybe one day their life will depend upon what you did while you were here.

In October of 1957, Danny Thomas asked if I would help him. Trudy responded for me, "Danny, Jim will be with you all the way."

She was very convincing and my life changed from that moment on.

God bless you all.
He loves you and so do I,

Jim Maloof,
Peoria, Illinois
Sunday, September 26, 2010

About Jim Maloof

Jim Maloof is widely recognized as one of the original 12 Founding Fathers of ALSAC - the American Lebanese Syrian Associated Charities.

ALSAC is the fundraising arm of St. Jude Children's Research Hospital in Memphis, Tennessee. ALSAC is responsible for raising the $1.5 million dollars per day it cost to operate St. Jude today.

He is the chairman of the board and founder of St. Jude Children's Research Hospital Midwest Affiliate clinc, the first of its kind anywhere in the world. And on July 20, 2010, the affiliate was renamed The Jim and Trudy Maloof Midwest Affiliate Clinc.

From 1985 to 1997, he served as Mayor of Peoria, Illinois, his hometown.

Jim is also the founder of Jim Maloof Realty, one of the largest realtors in downstate Illinois.

At 91 years of age he shows no sign of slowing down and still goes to work everyday.

James Aloysius Maloof: Curriculum Vitae

Honors: Institution named after

The Jim and Trudy Maloof Midwest Affiliate clinic

Honors: Other

Emertis Board Member — St. Jude Children's Research Hospital

Honorary "Sister" Member of Epsilon Sigma Alpha Sorority

Honorary Lifetime Member — Peoria Park District

Honorary Lifetime Member — The American Legion

Friedrichshafen Honorary Citizen Award

Honorary Member Italian American Society

Honorary Member — Bradley University Alumni

Masonic:

Jim is a member of the Temple Lodge No. 46, Scottish Rite Valley of Peoria, and Mohammed Temple, Shrine.

In September 2000, Jim was awarded the Thirty-third Degree at the annual meeting in Pittsburgh, P.A. This is the highest honor of Scottish Rite Masonry.

Founder:

St. Jude Children's Research Hospital Midwest Affiliate, Methodist Medical Center in Peoria, Illinois

Established

The Jim Maloof Endowment for the Peoria Ballet 2010- present

The Jim Maloof / Realtor Scholarship for Bradley University 1977-1983

Awards:

*Pope John Award

*B'Nai B'Rith Man of the Year: cited in the Congressional Record

*Special Recognition by the State of Illinois — Gov. Jim Edgar

*Others Award and *Service Award- Salvation Army

*Helen Haien Good Samaritan Award — South Side Mission

*Distinguished Service Award — Peoria Rescue Ministries

*Good Eagle Scout Award — Boy Scouts of America

*Land of Lincoln Award

*Kiwanis Tri-County Man of the Year

*Kiwanis — Louis V. Amador Medallion Award

*Legion of Honor — South-West Kiwanis

*Midwest Federation — American Syrian Lebanese Clubs Award

*Service Award — 500 Club for Lebanon

*YMCA Appreciation of Youth Award

*The Jefferson Award

*Patriotism Award — U.S. Marine Corps

*County Old Settlers Association Award

*Governor's Citation Award, State of Illinois Better Community Life

*Silver Good Citizenship Medal — Son of the American Revolution

*Service Award — Peoria Federation of Teachers

*Service Award — American Legion

*Knight of the Month — Knights of Columbus

*Award of Excellence — Center for Independent Living

*Appreciation Award — Low Income Housing

*1980 Boss of the Year Peoria Chater Chapter ABWA

*Peoria Observer Enterprise Award

*Tom Connor Award

*Junior Achievement Award

*Appeciation Award — Zeller Chapel, Zeller Clinic

Service: Served on/as

Honorable Mayor of Peoria, Illinois 1985-1997

Chairman of the Board — St. Jude Children's Hospital Midwest Affiliate

Past-President — St. Jude Children's Hospital Midwest Affiliate

Chairman of the Peoria, Illinois, St. Jude Telethon

National Executive 1st Vice President of ALSAC

National Executive 2nd Vice President of ALSAC

Nationa Executive 3rd Vice President of ALSAC

Member of the Executive Management Board of Directors,
St. Jude Children's Research Hospital, Memphis, Tennessee

Original Member of the Peoria Civic Center Commission

Chairman / Legislative Committee — Illinois Municipal League

Illinois Human Rights Commission

Past-President Kiwanis Club South-West Peoria

Chairman of Christian Education Fund Drive — St. Philomena Parish

Chairman of Bradley University Athletic Fund Drive

Master of Ceremonies of the Annual Christmas Sing

Board of Directors	Methodist Medical Center Foundation
Board of Directors	Peoria Symphony
Board of Directors	YMCA
Board of Directors	Creve Coeur Club
Board of Directors	ICR — Inter Community Relocation
Board of Directors	Economic Development Council
Board of Directors	Peoria Area Chamber of Commerce
President	Peoria Ballet
Member	Orpheus Club
Member	Mohammed Temple Shrine
Member	Kiwanis South-West
Member	Knights of Columbus
Member	American Legion

Go Help the Children & God Help You

Acknowledgments

We would like to extend a special thank you to all of those who made this book possible.

First of all, we would like to thank our Lord and Savior for His grace and His mercy.

With special acknowledgement of the contributions of the following:

James Aloysius Maloof

I would like to thank my loving daughter **Janice Maloof** for taking such good care of me every single day. I don't know how I'd get by without you.

It would take another book to mention all of the corporations who annually provide resourses for the 100+ St. Jude events hosted in Central Illinois every year.

There are a few which are on my heart at this moment and I feel compelled to mention them. A special thank you goes to **Caterpillar** for their generous and continued support; and thank you to State Farm Insurance, led by **Mike Davidson** and **Kevin Callis**.

A big warm thank you to **Kroger** for providing food for just about all of the events, and thanks to **Mike Joseph** and all the Kroger employees who prepare the meals.

Also, thank you to **Pekin Insurance**, led by **Scott Martin** and their "special angels" whose examples of giving are truly a God send.

For their wonderful efforts in helping to save the lives of cancer stricken children, I thank God for them all.

Douglas E. Love

I would like to thank my employer **P.A. Bergner & Co.** for giving me extended time off to work on this project, with a special thank you to my Assistant Store Manager, **Kelli Scott-Xanos** for making it happen.

Emily Hathway, thank you for willingness to transcribe all the interviews, without you this project would have never gotten off the ground.

A special thank you to my mom, **Judy Love**, this book was your idea, many, many years ago. I hope you enjoy it. You've been a constant cheerleader, helpful proof reader, and wonderful friend.

The same goes for my sister, **Chris Love**. Thank you for diligently reading and re-reading the manuscript over and over again in all of its different forms.

I would also like to thank **Janice Maloof** for her constant encouragement and for providing the all these wonderful family photographs - absolutely fabulous.

Thanks to **Dr. Rachel Dellinger** and **Yann Noirot** for reading the text and sharing their keen insights; and to **Cynthia J. Gysin** for photographing the special memorabilia at Jim's office.

Also my heartfelt appreciation goes out to the **Clay Johnson Family**; the **Amy McClellan-Jones Family**; and **the Family of Dusty Paulter** for allowing Jim to share their stories. Thank you for sharing your family photographs, they are very special.

A special shout out goes to my early educators **Mr. Gene Beltz** and **Mrs. Darlene Dyer** for putting the passion for the word in my blood; and to **Mike Shirey** and **Garth Cushman**.

And lastly, thanks to **Marshall Lipkin** who introduced Jim and I to each other, just over two years ago, with this project specifically in mind.

About Douglas E. Love

Douglas E. Love currently writes theater reviews for *The Live Theatre League of Central Illinois*. And you can hear him read his reviews on WCBU radio.

He has covered the Arts & Entertainment scene in and around the Peoria area since 2000, writing for *The Peoria Times-Observer*, *The Village Constitution*, and *The Peoria County News Bulletin*.

Love scripted *The Koerner Wedding Celebration* for the Peoria Park District. This 1860's historical re-enactment was named one of the best local events of 2004 by *The Peoria Journal Star*.

A graduate from Bradley University with a degree in Literature and the Creative Imagination, Love plans on continuing his education. He would like to attend seminary and work in the field of Christian Counseling.

He has written one book of poetry, *Martyr* (1990), and four Chapbooks. His poems have appeared in national publications such as *Black Dirt Magazine*, and *The New Poetry Review*.

He is also an employee of P.A. Bergner & Co.

Healthy Kids Helping Sick Kids: *(left to right)* **Chris Love**, **Doug Love**, and **Kim Pinter** present Dr. Hart with a check to the St. Jude Midwest Affiliate.

Help us raise $$$ for St. Jude

By Sharing your favorite Jim Maloof story with us.

What you have read here are some of Jim's favorite stories, but we bet you have some of your own you'd like to tell.

why not share yours in our next book

Maloof Memories

Send your story to

Love Publishing Ink
c/o Maloof Memories
P.O. Box 10288
Peoria, Illinois 61612-0288

Submissions should be limited to 200 words or less.
All submissions, including photographs become the property of Love Publishing Ink.
Submission must be postmarked by July 31, 2011 for consideration.
Please include your name, address, a daytime phone number,
and your relationship to Jim Maloof.
If you would like to include a photograph with you submission,
please be sure it is a copy, they will not be returned.

If you would like to join us in our fight to defeat childhood cancer

please, won't you *make a donation* to

The Jim & Trudy Maloof Midwest Affiliate clinic

checks should be made out to
St. Jude Children's Research Hospital

all donations are tax deductible

Mail your generous gift of love to

**The Jim & Trudy Maloof Midwest
Affiliate clinic
530 Northeast Glen Oak Avenue
Peoria, Illinois 61603**

Mike McCoy,
past-president of the St. Jude Midwest Affiliate clinic

Go Help the Children & God Help You